'It's no mystery or se...
Ch...

'If you were obses...
were competing on L...
want to get yourse...

'Hilarious . . . gives a fresh perspective on the
autobiographical drag queen format. Lawrence shares
some of her most intricate and personal stories, as well
as her extremely professional opinion on various subjects
such as concocting a drag name, mental health,
and dating.' – *Gay Times*

'Our fabulous queen has arrived. Go Lawrence!'
– Douglas Scott, author of *Shuggie Bain*

'A candid look back at Lawrence's journey so far – their
difficult childhood, marred by bullying; their painfully
relatable coming out story; their journey towards better
mental health. It's not all serious – there are hilarious, NSFW
sex stories, insights into the *Drag Race UK* werk room, and
a practical guide on how to become – as the title
suggests – a drag superstar.' – *Pink News*

'Tackles everything from gender identity, the thrill of a
wig and why Scottish talent is often overlooked.' – *i News*

'Fantastic . . . feisty, opinionated, and honest.' – *Daily Record*

'Full of one-liners and charm, this cheery memoir comes
complete with valuable life lessons and tricks of the
trade. Absolutely fabulous fun.' – *Best Magazine*

'With sky-high wigs and pin-sharp wit, Lawrence is one
of the UK's most loved drag acts. Here the season two
winner of *RuPaul's Drag Race UK* explains how humour
is a lifesaver.' – *Daily Express*

www.penguin.co.uk

LAWRENCE CHANEY

Drag QUEEN OF SCOTS

Life lessons on paint, pride and padding

PENGUIN BOOKS

TRANSWORLD PUBLISHERS
Penguin Random House, One Embassy Gardens,
8 Viaduct Gardens, London SW11 7BW
www.penguin.co.uk

Transworld is part of the Penguin Random House group of companies
whose addresses can be found at global.penguinrandomhouse.com

First published in Great Britain in 2021 by Bantam Press
an imprint of Transworld Publishers
Penguin paperback edition published 2022

A CIP catalogue record for this book
is available from the British Library.

ISBN
9780552178884

Typeset in Garamond by Jouve (UK), Milton Keynes.
Printed and bound in Great Britain by Clays Ltd, Elcograf S.p.A.

The authorized representative in the EEA is Penguin Random House Ireland,
Morrison Chambers, 32 Nassau Street, Dublin D02 YH68.

Penguin Random House is committed to a sustainable
future for our business, our readers and our planet. This book
is made from Forest Stewardship Council® certified paper.

I want to not only dedicate this book to
my grandmother, but also thank her:
Mary – the wee purple blob!

Contents

1

Welcome to My World

Och aye the noo! It's me, Lawrence Chaney, winner of *RuPaul's Drag Race UK*. If you've picked up this book, you probably know me as the purple-clad goddess who's been captivating audiences across the nation. Or maybe you've just heard people screaming 'LAW-WWWWHRENCE CHAAAANEH!!!' at their TV screens in a shite Scottish accent.

Either way, you're here now, and with my *Drag Race* journey coming to an end and Hollywood on the horizon, I wanted you all to get to know me a wee bit better. You've seen me walk runways and slay a challenge or three, but now it's time to open the lid on the drag world and how I found my way to international stardom.

People are always asking for advice on how to get started and how to further themselves, so I thought I'd compile a complete guide to doing so. This book is part autobiographical, part self-help book, and it's going to cover it all, from how to paint your face to how to deal with those shady queens (and I don't just mean their five o'clock shadow). It's for my fans but also for anyone wanting to follow in my footsteps. Not just wee Scottish queens, but anyone from a small town who aspires bigger than the sheep that they see out of their back window.

It'll also be packed to the brim with tales from my early days. I have had many ups and downs throughout my career and wanted to be frank with you all. This thing didn't happen overnight. There were a lot of obstacles to overcome. I've taken this opportunity to share many of my mishaps, so you don't have to make the same mistakes – and there are some corkers, believe me. Going from being the little Helensburgh wean who started drag with nothing but a set of feather lashes and a dream to becoming the UK's next *Drag Race* superstar is no easy feat. *Drag Race* has changed my life for ever and so have the queens that I shared the stage with, so I want to tell my story.

For me, 'drag' is a very broad term, because a lot of things fit under the umbrella of 'drag'. A lot of our community could still be considered 'underground', but you'll see drag pop up constantly, even in places you might not expect! However, don't worry, even though I want to talk about the good and the bad, this book won't be full of sob stories and crying . . . I did enough of that on *Drag Race*!

Here you'll find valuable life lessons and tricks of the trade that I have learned through doing or in some cases not doing. The goal for a lot of queens out there is to be thrust into RuPaul's bosom and be shown off to the world! (I'd be fine with just RuPaul's bosom.) For all you *Drag Race* superfans, I can't wait to give you the insider scoop on what really goes on in that Werk Room. Behind the catfights and spotlights there is a lot of love and positivity, something we could all do with a good dose of. There'll also be plenty of laughs, mostly at my expense, and a sprinkling of shade in there for good measure. You'll get the full experience with me, babes! Or at least, that's what it says on my Grindr profile anyway.

Of course there's more to drag than wigs and make-up (though don't worry, I've got you covered there). I get into the nitty-gritty of my mental health, too. I know what you are thinking: *We've seen enough on the TV.* Well, that was just the tip of the iceberg, hen! I'll also be telling you all about what it's like to go dating as a drag queen – which, by the way, is a lot more depressing than you'd think, and I know half of you already think it's pretty depressing. I've opened my heart (and legs) up to give you a look at my tragic dating experiences and flop relationships (pun intended). I might not have cracked the code for true and undying love, but I can show you how to not smudge your lipstick when eating a Big Mac!

I want to offer a unique perspective on what it's like to meander your way through life without letting the bad shit hold you back. I was the weird arty kid in school, with a bowl cut, who somehow turned into an international drag superstar. I'm going to take you through each valuable step of my journey in the hope that it inspires you to start yours.

I was nervous about writing this book because, first of all, hen, I barely read. But second, because I've heard so many stories about how authors have been censored and I want to be as authentic as possible. If you think you can censor Lawrence Chaney, you have another thing coming. You can trust that this book is me at my most honest – basically because I have too many enemies who will expose my arse if I try and fabricate shit. After some heated negotiations with my publisher, I'm only allowed to say 'fuck' five times, and I was told explicitly that I can only have three cunts in the book: the one writing it, the one approving it and you, the one reading it! I think that's what they meant anyway. I've definitely exceeded my limit, so don't grass me up to the publishers or I'll never get a book two.

The suits at Penguin have also advised that some people might not be able to understand some of my Scottishness. To keep them happy, I've created a glossary at the end of the book with all the Scottish-isms and drag terms you need to understand. If you ever find yourself stuck, just flip back there and you'll be fine. If I'm being as authentic as possible, this means I won't be watering down that Scottish twang. One thing I pride myself on is being unapologetically myself, even if this means ruffling a few feathers along the way. Look at it this way. You'll learn a lot of new fun phrases to shout at strangers in the street.

I hate it when autobiographies gloss over the truth and only show experiences through a rose-tinted lens. I've come here to tell it like it is. This is the full Lawrence Chaney truth and nothing but the truth (so help me God). I've made mistakes and I've learned from some experiences in the past, and I want to talk about them openly. I know there are many young queer kids out there who have watched me on *Drag Race* and resonated with my story. This book is for you lot. I want to show you that you can do whatever you set your mind to. It has taken me a long time to learn to ignore the bullies and be kind to myself. I hope my advice helps you cut some corners on your own path to acceptance and self-love. This one is also for all my Scottish gals out there. I'm living proof that we can hit the big time.

What we all need right now is a good laugh and a massive helping of love in this world and Lawza's here to give it to you, because as the great undiscovered recording artist known as RuPaul once said: 'A little bit of love goes a long long way'!

So, without further ado, let's get cracking.

2

Becoming Lawrence Chaney

My humble beginnings are as good a place to start as any. I may only be a wee youth, but a lot has happened to bring me to where I'm at now.

I want to say this chapter is a whistlestop tour of my adolescence into adulthood, but I'm afraid you're getting the *full* Chaney experience – so buckle up, it's going to be a bumpy ride! From defeating school bullies to dealing with loss, coming out and my body image, I didn't realize just how formative those years growing up were, in terms of becoming the legend I am today!

To Helensburgh and Beyond

I was born in Helensburgh, a small seaside town about forty minutes from Glasgow, where not much happens beyond the charity-shop wars. It's got lovely picnic spots, but in general it's a bit of a closed-minded place.

I lived there with my mum Phyllis, my father Nick and my sister Tamsin. I was a happy-go-lucky kind of kid who enjoyed a bit of dressing-up here and there. The furthest I strayed away from being a 'normal kid' was trying on my mum's eyeliner.

Aside from this, life was pretty bog standard at this point. We spent the first nine years of my life in this town, until my dad got a job in England. He left the Navy for some fancy new career and we were all dragged along with him. To this day, I still don't really know what his job is. It's just one of those standard dad jobs, where they do man things. All I know is it's not a career path I'll be going down any time soon.

We moved from one shitey wee town to another and right oot of my comfort zone. This was a monumental move, as it was the first time I'd been outside of Scotland, and we ended up in a wee town just outside of Reading called Newbury. In the words of Tiffany Pollard, it was an old-maiden type of town, a town that I wouldn't have picked out for myself.

When I was just starting school, there wasn't much bullying going on. I think it's because when you're a kid you're all weirdos with bowl cuts and Velcro trainers from Shoe Zone, so you are naturally a bit less judgemental. I think the most extreme insult I got in primary school was being called a nerd. The most trouble I got in was for writing the word 'fuck' down on a piece of paper. Yes, from day dot

Lawrence Chaney was a foul-mouthed little bitch. My mum was called by the school, it was a whole palaver, but the shame from this experience meant I didn't write another fuck down on paper for many years.

It was hard to find a new school for me when we first moved to England. I was a creative kid and wanted somewhere that would support that. We eventually chose a school called The Willows. Spending these very formative years in an alien environment made it difficult to carve out my identity. I'd like to say the first few years there were relatively uneventful, but immediately the kids learned how to judge, and the bullying began.

Being the only Scottish one in the room was tough, because as soon as you open your mouth you stick out like a sore thumb.

I suppose it's a bit like being on *Drag Race UK*; I was a Scottish icon surrounded by English people who couldn't understand me. Sadly, I didn't have Ellie Diamond by my side to make me look like the more talented, gorgeous, beautiful and *thin* one this time. If you are a Scottish person in England, you'll feel my pain. The number of subtle differences between these neighbouring nations is astronomical, even at a young age.

If I wasn't getting slagged off for the way I pronounced certain words, I was getting compared to the character Fat Bastard from *Austin Powers*. At the time, the Scottish characters in the collective consciousness were Fat Bastard, Susan Boyle and Shrek . . . So aye, you can imagine the insults.

I'd have done anything to shake off these silly comparisons when I was a kid, but now I think that trio sounds like my dream dinner-party guest list. At The Willows I was called every name under the sun, but of all the slurs thrown my way, 'fat ginger cunt' was the most cutting. This was largely because I am not, and never have been, ginger, so you can understand my outrage. Yes, I was a flat-footed weirdo with Lego hair, so I don't blame them for giving me grief, but I draw the line at 'ginger'. Not that I have a problem with being ginger, but because it is factually inaccurate. If you are going to insult me, please make it something to which I can reply, 'Fair enough actually, cannae deny that one!'

People would also call me 'ginger pubes'. I was nine years old. I had not a pube in sight. Where's the quality control?

There was a part of straight people's mentality that I was already at odds with, from the get-go. I just never aligned with the way they fitted the mould. I never had any interest in the clothes they wore or the music they listened to. I didn't share the same aspirations as them or watch the shows they watched. It creates a kind of othering environment. I wanted to listen to show tunes, not Eminem. The only 'Eminems' I cared about were the peanut chocolate ones.

The constant name-calling made me go from the kid wearing jazz pants and dancing to Liza Minnelli to an introvert who struggled to express themselves. I isolated myself by staying at home and watching *Doctor Who*, something I took a lot of comfort from when I didn't want to leave the house. The reason I resonate with *Doctor Who* so much is because the Doctor is an outsider. They're able to travel to all these different planets with all these aliens on them. Some are enemies, some are peaceful, but they don't care. It's about who they are as a person (or monster); not their skin colour, not what they sound like . . . I love that message. It is bizarre that such a fantasy realm actually resonates with the real world so much.

But as much as I resisted, when Monday came around it was back to the wrath of my bullies.

There was one stand-out occasion during my final year of primary school, when I was ten years old. A boy in my year had rallied up all of my classmates and instructed them to take off their school jumpers, whirl them up and whack me over the head with them in the playground. This was my full class attacking me. Can you imagine what that felt like? When there was a full class of rampant weans attacking you and your teacher couldn't do anything about it (she'd have to pull up the whole class), it fucks you up a bit. I've finally worked through my feelings of victimization, but you cannae blame me for taking a while to do so.

My trust in people really took a battering, and this is something I'm still trying to get my head around. Listen, people can be lovely, but people can also have jumpers they can whirl up and whack at you!

This was also around the same time that I started struggling with my body image. I don't need to convince you that PE was every gay's nightmare. As far as I'm concerned, it was just an excuse for the straights to bully the queer kids and nerds and call it 'exercise'. Don't even get me started on the so-called sport of dodgeball, or British Bulldog as it was called at The Willows. That shit should be illegal. I've never been so afraid of catching balls in all my life.

High School, Low Self-esteem

I continued on to high school in Newbury. I attended Park House Secondary School and Sports College. *Sports College.* (I know what you're thinking, but they had a banging photography and art department.) I stayed there for three years.

For the first time, I had two close friends. I was still shy but was able to open up to them a bit more and it was such a relief to find actual mates. But it wasn't long before their other friends were calling me a fat Scottish cunt and they didn't know what to do, because they were so used to blending in. What were they meant to do when a friend of theirs stood out? Looking back at it, I don't blame them. High school is tough and you need to survive it any way you can. At the time, I found myself getting more angsty and aggressive, so I withdrew inside myself, letting fewer and fewer people in.

In January 2010, my grandmother passed away and we were all absolutely devastated. My gran was a big part of my life. We used to call her 'the wee purple blob' because she always wore lilac, smelled like lavender and shuffled about the place like a wee orb. She lived with us in England, which was great, because we got to look after her and spend a lot more time together.

Mary was always encouraging me to express myself. She taught me how to paint (on paper) and really nurtured my creativity. Every birthday present she bought for me would be art-based. Whether that would be paints, pencils, pottery kits, sketchbooks, all of it allowed me to explore that side of myself that would later on serve me so well in my career.

A huge sadness in my life is that my grandmother never got to see any of my success in drag. I know she would've been so proud. She is, of course, why my favourite colour is purple and why you see it used in so many of my looks. I decided to carry on my gran's purple reign and still do so to this day. This one is for you, Mary, my wee purple blob.

As our whole family was devastated, my parents took time off work, and my sister and I took some time off school when she passed away. As it always did, the news got back to my classmates that my gran had died. I thought that maybe I'd be met with some compassion and sympathy. I was at such a low point, I couldn't really take facing any more hardships at school. But kids know just how to kick you when you're down.

On my first day back, on the whole, people were very sympathetic and supportive because of the loss of my gran. I think losing a grandparent is something we all have experience of, and they often would confide in me about their losses. This gave me a shoulder to lean on and was a comforting contrast to previous experiences. But there is always one bastard, isn't there?

I remember vividly queuing up outside of art class with the rest of my year, and this wee toerag said to me that he was going to piss on my gran's grave. He had crossed the line. After a build-up of so much shit, this was something that I just couldn't cope with. I just saw red in this moment. Cue the *Kill Bill* sirens.

Now, I am not a violent person by any means, but that day I got into the first fight of my life, and to everyone's surprise, including my own, I gave him a bit of a doing-in. He was definitely shocked. Up until this point I'd resisted fighting back with anything other than words, but this time I had to stand up for myself. It was primal. Feeding time at the zoo.

This was my first experience of fighting back and it did a lot more than asking teachers for help ever did. This is something I hope schools have managed to change for the better – kids shouldn't need to take matters into their own hands, or be using their own hands for that matter. I had begun telling myself that it was better to confront the bullies myself and deal with the consequences rather than ask for help from the people in charge. Yikes. That's right, wee Lawrence, the baby Terminator.

No way was my maw, Big Phyllis, going to sit back while that school turned me into a cage-fighter. She pulled up to the school to have a stern word with the headteacher. I'm making my mum out to be Scarface here. She is a really lovely woman. Just don't mess with her family.

The bullies had made my life hell, and the teachers didn't help me, which only made me feel worse. I was at a real loss and this is where a lot of my issues with trust and relationships started.

Bullying is a learned behaviour, totally preventable, so it is a shame that kids end up taking that path. Teachers need to be better equipped to deal with it too. Section 28 has been in the bin for years!

The whole situation created a horrible atmosphere at home because I just wasn't happy, and I began closing off to my parents and taking it out on them too. My parents prioritized my wellbeing and decided to make the big move back up to Scotland. So here we were, back in Helensburgh . . . again. They found work (Dad got another big-boy job) and there you have it.

I started fourth year at Hermitage Academy. This was the secondary school that linked on from my OG primary school, so obviously a lot of people I went to primary school with were there. Naively, I thought I would be accepted by said people. At least they were Scottish. Surely I'd fit in here? I had some friends from primary school that I thought I'd be able to link back up with, but this sadly wasn't the case.

Naturally, these old friends had grown up and changed over the years, just like I had. We no longer had a lot in common and didn't fit into the same social cliques. For example, they were aw aboot Dungeons and Dragons, and I was aw aboot the Dungeons and Drag Queens. High school is difficult and kids do what they have to do for survival, and if that means conforming to fit into a certain group that keeps you from sticking out and getting bullied, then often that comes at the expense of old friendships.

Starting in a new place, halfway through secondary school, is difficult – everyone's all set with their friend-ship groups and they don't want to open ranks to the newbie – who, incidentally, still had a bowl cut. I started being tripped up in corridors, laughed at for the way I looked or walked. It was like I was back at square one.

It got to the point where I had to go home at lunchtimes. The bell would go and my mum would be outside, waiting to whisk me away, with a cheese toastie waiting at home. I once again began retreating further into myself. My mum tried all she could to get me to open up and talk about how I felt, or give me advice on how to make friends or how to just get through the school year. I appreciated that, but it just felt so far off . . . I didn't know how I'd last to the end of the school year without friends.

Latterly, in fourth year, I made a few acquaintances – a girl called Josie who sat across from me in Maths, a girl called Constance and an out and proud queerdo called Liam. This was when it dawned on me that I had more in common with women than any men (sorry, Liam). I started to get to know these people throughout the year, but I was not hanging out with them just yet – we had a few common interests (Lady Gaga, obvs). It was fifth year when everything changed.

Picture it. RE class. 2012. The world hadn't ended. This one guy threw a Bible at my head and people started laughing, and I thought, *Fuck it*, and chucked the holy book back at him. The blasphemy. I know.

As I launched it straight at his head, I said, 'This is the second coming, arsehole!' and the class erupted with laughter.

Even the guy who threw the book at me initially started laughing, saying it was fair play. For the first time they were laughing *with* me, not at me, and I felt incredible.

I had allowed myself to become so closed-off to the people in my school that they just belittled me. Finally, something within me broke. I utilized the sense of humour I had been suppressing and not showing anyone – even my parents for the past few years. It felt like I was coming out the closet . . . as a comedian.

Overnight, my status in school changed. Suddenly I was a legend.

It dawned on me that my natural sense of humour was my ticket out of this cycle of bullying. It allowed me to see myself through a new lens and finally gain acceptance. The humour and ability to read people became synonymous with my drag. It's all linked. This is a perfect example of how you can take a bad experience and flip it on its head. I learned to be funny as a defence mechanism and eventually it led me to create my drag persona, which is rooted in comedy. This is why I say drag is not just a job for me, it was my only way out.

Struggling with my self-image has shaped me into the funny person I am today. I find it very easy to laugh at myself and I think this is something you develop through hardship. Being the funny one is a massive defence mechanism. To avoid being slagged off, I'd make people laugh with my razor-sharp clap-backs. I'd channel this fake confidence and be a bit cheeky to those that were on my case. I'd also make jokes at my own expense, about my outfits, hair, gayness. You name it, I was taking the piss out of it. When my peers realized I was actually quite funny, they respected me a bit more.

This kept the wolves at bay for a bit. Once you've used that mechanism to survive, you realize: *Hold on a minute, I'm actually quite funny.* Then you can use it to your own advantage. You can take all that pain and discomfort and turn it into a positive. I used it as a springboard to go out and entertain the masses. If everyone processed trauma in this way, we'd have a lot more joy and love in the world. It's important to remember that these bad experiences do not define you, but they're just part of life.

Sure, it would have been nicer if I didn't have to go through all of the bullying and hardships, but I can't change the past. I can only use the experience to better myself and make my mark on the world in a positive way. So I look back on a lot of bad experiences and realize they contributed to my personality and allowed me to look at life differently. I'm a very observant person, and being able to sit back and observe the nuances of people's personalities has allowed me to create a comedic presence that people can relate to. Not to be all Kelly Clarkson here, but what doesn't kill you makes you stronger. Or actually, it makes you funnier.

Though I was relieved to finally be accepted by my

classmates, I was still very shy and knew that my new-found popularity would be ruined if I told anyone I was gay. I had seen the way people had spoken about and treated Liam for his sexuality and I can't believe so many people created problems with him . . . solely for being gay. They didn't even bother trying to fabricate a cover story: purely the fact that he took it up the shite chute was the deciding factor in his bullying experience.

I genuinely can't think of a time when I thought I was straight. I guess I didn't consider it at any point of my early life. I had never seen girls as people that I'd be in a relationship with, but that's also because I didn't consider being in a relationship with anyone. As many gay people will say, it was when the other boys started fancying the girls that you realized that you fancy the boys.

I was probably around ten or eleven when I first thought about it at all. I was genuinely too busy perfecting my cabaret dance routine to take love and relationships into consideration. When you go through puberty, it's like zero to a hundred, really fast. Suddenly you fancy every man that lays eyes on you. Thank God this is a short-lived phase, otherwise I'd have ended up married with ten kids by now.

I found it easier to be under the radar and make everyone laugh than to come out and end up hiding again, going home for lunch and not being seen or heard. I eventually became the class clown that even the teachers liked. Things had really turned around, but I knew I was still concealing a big part of myself, which started to take a toll.

Despite being in a better place for the remainder of my high-school years, things were still a bit shite. To give you an idea, my best pal was a fabulous art and photography teacher and I spent most of my break times hanging about in her classroom. If you didn't dodge a game of football with the other lads to spend your lunchtimes hanging around in a dingy room with a slightly kooky middle-aged woman, are you really gay? I don't think so.

Mrs McKay, if you're reading this, you're a legend and I hope you're thriving. Art, Drama and English teachers are the fierce protectors of weird kids, so I salute them all for having our backs. This lunchtime refuge was the only place where I felt free to be Lawrence in all their camp glory. I could express myself freely with someone who encouraged and praised the part of my personality that I was otherwise encouraged to get rid of. Chatting about art, music, films and Madonna with my teacher was one of the first instances when I realized other people liked the same shit that I did.

By the time it came to sixth year, prom was looming. I felt empowered and decided I wanted to go in drag. I'd been playing dress-up for a while by this point, in the safety of my own home. I was well on the way to becoming a *RuPaul's Drag Race* superfan, and like most of my obsessions, I have to go all-in with them. There is nothing in my life that I do in half-measures. So now that I was obsessed with drag and actually understood what it was, I thought: *When's a better time to debut than prom?*

I was obsessed with over-the-top dresses, lace beading, the little sewing poof inside me loved it all. Prom seemed like gay Christmas to me. I was pretty adamant about it at the time, but in hindsight I understand why some teachers had their reservations about it. As my guardian angel, Mrs McKay strongly advised against it. It was upsetting to hear her discouraging me. She was a cool gal and this protest didn't make sense to me. I thought she would've been right up for it.

There was a lot of back and forth and I changed my mind a hundred times. After all her advice about embracing my individuality, I couldn't understand why I shouldn't make this courageous step. Ultimately, she knew that I would've gotten my arse handed to me by the bullies, so she ended up putting her foot down to protect me, and I ended up skipping prom altogether. If you won't accept me at prom in a frock, then quite frankly I think you're a cock.

For all you teens out there, prom really isn't the be all and end all. I had a fab time watching horror movies with my alt friend Miriam instead. It may sound like I've stolen this friendship dynamic straight from Damian and Janis in *Mean Girls*, but as far as I'm concerned, they stole it from me. Come at me, Tina Fey. I'm a firm believer that real icons never went to prom. I know that I would've been heckled by the straight boys or been tripped over in my two-inch heels (an ASDA special), but I didn't care. I definitely would've been the talk of the town, literally, if I'd turned up in a dress and heels. But part of me wishes I had just said 'Fuck it, I'm going anyway!'

So if someone wants to throw me a prom now, please do, but I'm only coming if I get guaranteed prom queen. The *Drag Race* crown may have filled a void, but a queen can never have too many crowns.

Just before going away to film *Drag Race*, I was invited back to Hermitage Academy in Helensburgh and I got the chance to meet the newly formed LGBTQ+ society there. It was so inspiring to see this generation of queer kids taking measures into their own hands to ensure their safety and right to express themselves. There, I met a young drag queen named Ahria. To paint a picture, myself and her standing side by side looked like Naomi Smalls meeting Krusty the Clown. I later found out she had gone to her prom in drag. She was incredibly brave and talented, and no doubt took her prom by storm. I can't believe there was such a full-circle moment in such a short amount of time. She felt safe enough to do what I couldn't and go to prom in drag . . . Either that or Mrs McKay was on the payroll as her personal bodyguard.

I'm Coming Out

In Helensburgh, I had never been exposed to much freedom of expression. It's a place with a lot of character but a staunch small-town mentality. One of my best pals, Miriam, was a bit alternative, so to me she was the closest to a drag sister I had when growing up. She wore heavy make-up, was never seen without an ombré brow and bleached her roots at least twice a week. She dressed however the fuck she wanted. What I loved about her was that when I studied photography in school, she was a great model and was up for absolutely everything. She was a total free spirit and that's exactly what teenage Lawrence needed.

Imagine the power we would have if drag queens and the alternative community joined forces. We are more similar than you think! We're both outcasts from society, joining a band of misfits to feel accepted, and we both struggle with body odour. Hey, you try staying fresh while wearing a corset: it ain't easy!

My journey into drag wasn't complicated. I had been playing with my mum's make-up and heels since I can remember. Phyllis's Dream Matte Mousse taught me the ropes of make-up back in the day. I actually started doing drag first, before I came out as gay: it was a bit backwards. Despite all my fears of coming out, it went rather smoothly for me – probably because I waited until I was out of the hellhole that was my high-school environment and started attending the safe havens of the drag shows. I started seeing that you wouldn't be treated like my friend Liam was in school – there were places where queerness was encouraged, loved and celebrated. Other queens that I met told me of both their positive and negative experiences coming out, which led me to tell myself not to come out until I had a boyfriend.

It was like this: straight people don't need to come out whatsoever, so I didn't want to make waves until I had something to show for it. I decided that I wouldn't tell my family I was gay until I had a boyfriend. At the age of eighteen, lo and behold, I got one. I was doing a drag residency at the Rabbit Hole in Edinburgh at the time, and I felt like I was living a secret life. I'd say I was going to see my pal Alice Rabbit, when really I was donning fake tits on stage and dating my brand-new boyfriend! My mum knew I was doing drag, but she associated it with things like *Mrs Brown's Boys* and Dick Emery – straight men dressing up as women for a laugh. It was pure entertainment – which it is!

Only, a month into travelling to Edinburgh to meet my boyfriend and lying to my mum, I had to come clean. I was starting to panic about all the things that could happen to me that my mum wouldn't know about: what if some homophobic lowlifes put us in hospital? How could I explain on the phone to my mum if she thought I was away doing a show? I also had a terrible fear of coming home with a hickey. I don't ever want to have to address that situation with my mum or dad. I very much used the boyfriend as a springboard to come out to them.

I came out to my mum before my dad. Mums are our first best friends and confidantes, so they're generally the first choice when it comes to choosing who to spill your guts to.

She was incredibly supportive, loving and reassuring. It was the best experience I could've asked for, though I struggle with the general idea of even having to come out. It was 2015 – *Glee* already had six seasons out by then. Why did we still need to come out and make some big declaration? We don't need straight people to come out. I think the experience needs to be a bit more relaxed and casual.

I remember my mum picking me up on the first week of secondary school. She asked me 'Are there any boys or girls that you are interested in?' I thought this was a great way to be casual and laid back when it comes to sexuality. If you can make your children feel like they can be honest and not scared of how you will react, you are doing parenting right. (Despite this, I was still too feart and pretended I was straight, like a wee shitebag.)

When I think of the safe environment my mum created for me back then, I realize that Phyllis is a good egg and always has been. Everyone can take a leaf out of this book. I love my mum because she has a kind heart, she's caring and we are very similar people. This is what our relationship is founded on, not just on the fact we are blood related.

I actually came out to my sister before my mum because she was closer to my age and I thought she was more likely to understand. She wasn't the least bit fazed or surprised. Now it came to telling my mum. Even though I knew my mum was very supportive of queer people, you never know 100 per cent how something is going to go. I plucked up some courage, promised myself I wouldn't cry and said to Mum:

'Mum . . . I'm gay . . . I've got a boyfriend . . .'

Then what happened? I started to cry! She said everything I needed to hear.

'That's all right, Lawrence. We love you so much. Thank you for telling me.'

Whilst the relief of telling my mum was amazing, I still had to tell my dad, Big Nick. He was the one person I feared telling the most: Nick is a man of very few words, he only says about two a year. Mostly he communicates in grunts or by pointing. I remember asking my mum to tell my dad for me, hoping she'd act as a kind of buffer.

Nae luck. Mum insisted that I had to be the one to tell Dad – this was a huge part of my experience on this planet.

'This is your news to tell your father, not mine, but I'm here for you.'

I agreed, it probably would be better if I told him, so I got her to call Dad through to the front room. Her choice of words will stay with me for ever.

'*Nick!* Your son wants to tell you he's *gay*!'

It still makes me laugh to this day. She didn't think for a second that this was an odd way of letting him know, and that's what makes her the legend she is today.

After my mum basically came out for me, my dad walked into the living room and said 'Lawrence, let's go for a drive.'

I was bricking it because this was already four more words than Dad's yearly allowance. I thought he was going to drop me off in the countryside and tell me never to come back. We both felt awkward and we drove silently for a couple of miles before he said, 'So you have a boyfriend. Shall we have him over for dinner?'

I couldn't believe how fine he was with it. Like most things in life, all of your anxious thoughts and worries never seem to play out quite as badly as they did in your head. Of course things have been really shitty at times; and had this experience of coming out not gone as smoothly, I would've struggled, but I would've worked it out. You will realize how tenacious you are as a queer person early on in life.

Before I was ready to share being gay with everyone

else, I went through a period of coming to terms with it myself.

At first, I hated saying the word 'gay'. It was vomit-inducing to me. I wish it didn't affect me so much, but it was truly gut-wrenching. So many negative connotations came along with it. So many people, especially at school and in society in general, used the word 'gay' as an insult.

You go from *OK, maybe I fancy boys, but I would never actually be gay, I'm just a straight person who fancies boys*, to *OK,* maybe *I'm gay but I don't want to ever be in a relationship with a man and I'll just get married to a woman and live a 'normal' life.*

This then evolves into *I'm gay as fuck.*

Growing up in my family, where we are always joking and slagging each other off, it's hard to see where the joke ends and your true mindset lies. I was constantly reading into everything my family were saying about other gay people before I had come out. I was always trying to suss out what they really thought about being gay. I also realize now that I had internalized a lot of homophobia.

Looking back on it all, I would say if you are in the same position and are waiting for a partner to use to come out, you don't have to. It doesn't make you any more valid. If you can find the strength within yourself to do it without a relationship, the right people won't care. Of course I had some bad reactions, but none that really mattered to me. Random 'straight' boys from my schooldays still made the odd 'faggot' comment, but I've had the last laugh on many occasions when I've seen them pop up on Grindr.

It's a cliché to say that coming out is like lifting a huge weight off your shoulders, but it's true. When I moved to Glasgow in 2017, suddenly I was immersed even more in the scene, making friends who loved me for the part of myself I had hidden away for so long. When you realize how much you let something consume you, it is the ultimate relief when it's finally over. When you let go of shame and secrecy, you feel like a free wummin!

Like most small-town queens, where I grew up stunted my growth a little. Constantly having to hide who you are takes its toll on you. You're so far removed from the glitz and glamour of the big city, and you struggle to find where you fit.

I don't hold a grudge against anyone who passed judgement on my younger self. Don't get me wrong, the homophobic comments or whispered jibes in the school corridors stung like a bitch, but I realize now that behaviour like that stems from ignorance and a lack of exposure to anything that deviates from the 'norm'. I hope for future generations this continues to change. I am only young, and the changes for the queer community within my lifetime have already been monumental.

The Real Me

People often assume that a queen out of drag is 'the real you', but I've never looked at it that way. One of the biggest myths around drag is the belief that it confuses your identity, but this isn't always the case: for some, it solidifies it. Not to get all philosophical on you, but I've always seen Lawrence out of drag as a 'vessel'. This vessel has allowed me to fulfil my ambitions and dreams. Out of drag, I am like a blank canvas and I can use this to become whatever or whoever I want. I promise I'm not trying to be wanky here, it's just the best way I can explain how I feel. Being Lawrence Chaney on stage or on screen enables me to become whoever I want. Drag has allowed me to explore and embody figures I've idolized since childhood, from Madonna to Doctor Who! Ultimately, my performances are a product of everything that makes me uniquely me.

I think my name confuses people. They can't work out if I'm what they perceive to be a boy or a girl, and I don't blame them! I don't see gender binaries as a limiting factor in my drag or my everyday life. For some, drag allows them to explore their gender fluidity, whilst for others it helps them confirm their gender identity. Personally, I've found it to be a valuable tool for exploring who I truly am. It's pretty common for queens to struggle with how they are perceived out of drag, and we're often asked if we identify as transgender or non-binary. The answer is different from person to person of course, so as much as society would like to box us in, you can't make any sweeping assumptions about what drag means to an individual.

When it comes to gender identity, I've been through all the motions. There was a time when I thought I might be trans. When I was having these feelings in 2019, I sought out the advice of someone on the Glasgow drag scene. I confided in them in a McDonald's, where I like to hash (brown) out most of life's toughest decisions. I told them that I thought I might be trans and I didn't really know what it all meant. As a trans person themselves, I hoped they would offer me some advice or even point me in the right direction of where to go from here. I was shocked when this person said to me, 'I'm actually trans, more trans than you, don't ever forget it.'

Now, I don't know if this was a joke or not. Everyone around us looked puzzled and nervous-laughed. I was confused and this experience had such a negative impact on me. It completely invalidated my own experience and left me at a loose end. So was I not allowed to be trans? How do you define trans? Is there a scale? Do I have to take an exam? This encounter really knocked me back and has made me so hesitant to speak about my gender identity since.

I remember, during the broadcast of *Drag Race*, a lot of viewers were confused about what pronouns I used. RuPaul or Alan Carr would use 'he/him' to refer to me, Michelle would use 'she/her'. The process of discovering your gender identity doesn't happen overnight. The key message is that it's OK to not know. There is an expectation to work everything out at such a young age, and to be honest I haven't had much time to focus on it. I'm touring every single week and my life certainly isn't bliss. I'm turning my pants inside out on a tour bus and I still don't know if I am male, female, or somewhere outwith or in between. I think the best way to describe my gender is fluid, but this isn't finite. I see myself as ever evolving and always discovering more about myself.

There is a lot of pressure to be at the finish line. The same goes with any kind of journey. I know queens who have struggled with addiction and feel the same pressure to be at a point where they are looking back at their past as a whole new person. We are constantly changing, learning and evolving. I don't think this journey ever fully ends. So if you aren't where you want to be just yet, don't sweat it. As Miley Cyrus once said, it's all about the climb, babe. I've never climbed a mountain, and God knows I never will, but you get the essence of my point here.

For me, drag was used as a medium to empower myself. When I put that wig on, I feel my insecurities disappear. I was that oddball kid who struggled to find their place and people in my youth. It took me a while to find my band of misfits, but when I finally did, an overwhelming sense of pride kicked in. I realized . . . I'm Lawrence Chaney, bitch!

Having the opportunities to showcase my take on drag as an art form has given me the confidence to command a room. The thought of getting on any sort of stage couldn't have been further from my reality as a teen. If someone had told little Lawrence (well, not that little, I've always been a bit of a heifer) that I'd be on national television wearing a pair of fake tits and a face full of make-up, I'd have probably pished my drawers!

Despite knowing, deep down, that I wanted to explore a much more vibrant and exciting side of myself, it wasn't at all obvious to me how I could make that a reality. The gradual process of accepting who I truly was inside and out was made easier by embracing the artistry of drag and, in turn, stepping into my authenticity in ways I never could've imagined! This authenticity lends itself to my honest and self-deprecating humour, with my passion for drag being the pretty package I chose to wrap this up in. Through this self-acceptance I am able to poke fun at myself and not feel guilty about it. I can read myself a million times better than any other queen could – I pretty much consider myself a stand-up comedian with a few extra tricks up my sleeve.

Fattered: Fat and Shattered

Some of us have a great cake thrust upon us and what a blessing it is. Being a 'plus-size queen' has become a big part of my identity, through no choice of my own. As a bigger queen, you've been put in a box before you've even opened your mouth. This normally goes along with the assumption that you won't be a winner, which I am proud to have proved wrong!

Even in this day and age, people still discount you because of your appearance. I am so proud to be a bigger queen who has taken the *Drag Race* crown, because I want to show that your size has nothing to do with how capable or talented you are. We live in a society that constantly tells us we have to look a certain way and it can be disheartening to have this reinforced within the drag community, especially when we are supposed to be a group that uplifts each other and accepts our differences. I am one of the first ever big girls to take the crown and now is just as good a time as any.

When I first started drag, I wasn't anywhere near as talented as I am now, but I was skinnier. Another queen from the scene once showed me an old photo of a slimmer Lawrence and said, 'Och, what a shame, you had it all going for you back then.' This wasn't true at all. The me in that photo wasn't happy or confident, and also my lashes were crooked! My body was just a bit more palatable.

It takes a long time to love your body and this process isn't helped by reading comments about your appearance from people who don't know you. It is hard to accept that people sometimes seem to hate you purely because of your size. When people decide they don't like you before they've even got to know you, or are unkind on social media, it can sting. If you are someone whose weight has fluctuated throughout your life, you know first hand how people's attitudes towards you change when you are slimmer. In my experience, people suddenly value you a lot more when you drop a few pounds.

Don't get me wrong, we all love a compliment, and while most are well intentioned, it is hard to see people suddenly take an interest in your body when it's more conventionally attractive. Bottom line, I am the same person whether I am 'fat' or thin. It's easy to compare yourself to others, especially on the drag scene, and that's why the journey to self-love is all the more rewarding when you get there. Also, FYI to those who are partial to critiquing our bodies whilst in drag: half the time, I'm wearing ten tonnes of padding – you've no idea wit my body looks like! I could be shaped like a Rubik's cube for all you know!

Despite my unintentional branding as a 'plus-size queen', I've realized I want to wear it as a badge of honour. Drag has no set formula after all, so don't waste your time trying to fit a mould that your arse is too big for. I have spent a lot of time wanting to change myself and I can't tell you how liberating it is to just embrace every aspect of myself.

The Queen of Scots

Meeting my fellow Scottish drag artists was a huge part of becoming the confident Lawrence you all see today. There are so many exceptionally talented people in the Scottish scene, who are often overlooked. Being overlooked is something that bonds us together and the thing that lit the fire under my arse to work that bit harder! I was the first Scottish queen to walk into the Werk Room of *Drag Race UK*, and trust me, that's not something I take for granted. Being Scottish is a big part of who I am, not just a gimmick or a character. We Scots are a proud nation and it's about time our craft and place in the drag world was taken seriously.

When I was on the way to becoming a well-known name in the Scottish drag scene, my identity was strengthened by the validation you get from performing. Having a regular crowd of people who turn out to support you every week only builds confidence. That being said, Scotland is known for its ability to poke fun at people, which is great on the comedy scene but means that when it comes to breaking out of Scotland, you're not always met with the support you expect. There is an element of our culture that celebrates our natives when they are on the rise, but when they make it, people start to tear them down. It's almost like you can't get too big. If you surpass a level of local fame, you become a 'riddy' (you can flip to the glossary for all the Scottish slang definitions your heart desires). It's brutal how quickly the tides of opinion can turn.

The arts have always been full of talented Scots and it's not about to slow down any time soon. Ye cannae get rid of us, we're too loud! In an episode of *Drag Race*, RuPaul asked me if I had plans to move to London after the show. I meant what I said. I have no intention of doing that for the time being. I love Scotland and I love Glasgow. The problem is that all of the paid opportunities are elsewhere. We don't need more Scottish artists in London. We need Scottish artists to be taken seriously in Scotland. We have a vibrant, thriving scene here with so much potential.

It is often said that Scottish people don't become international superstars because people can't understand our accent. What a load of pish! The reason some people can't understand us is because they don't hear us enough. If a Scottish queen was on your telly every night, give it a week and you'll be fluent in Scots slang and reaching for the Irn-Bru. I have had supporters reach out from all over the world whilst on the show. When you have something authentic and stick to it, it resonates with people globally. I believe in embracing our identity and not trying to be something else in order to be seen.

3
Goodbye, Tallulah von Fuckbucket

Your name is your persona, it's your brand, and it's what you'll (hopefully) be seeing in lights one day! Working out a name that suits you is crucial, because your name becomes your identity – it will be on the T-shirts you flog and hollered at you by drunken fans when they see you after a show. Luckily, in this chapter I give away some expert advice on how to nail that all-important drag name and become the superstar you were born to be!

In short, it sticks with you for your entire career – if you've got one, that is. So please God, choose one that you actually like.

Choosing a Name

It's very easy to fall into the clichés of drag names (e.g. your Divines and O'Haras, or some sort of pun on drugs). If you want to pay tribute to a great queen that came before you by borrowing their surname, go for it. Just make sure that you have their approval or you could run into some bother down the line. Unless you are part of their official drag family, I would avoid doing this if you want to carve a professional career in drag. I would always suggest picking something that is true to you and maintains a sense of individuality. Trust me, I'm sure you will go through a few absolute shanners in the selection process.

Up and coming drag queens always want to know how I chose my name. Was there a list? Did I trial some different ideas first? Did I fly in a crack team of marketing professionals to help me come up with it? The answer to all of these questions is no: I chose the first drag name that came into my head. I'm not advising you do the same, though. I made it work, but not everyone can.

As most people know, my real name is Lawrence. Audiences seem to have a strange obsession with finding out your government name, so there you have it. I thought I'd keep half of my own identity and adopt another half from someone else.

I am a huge fan of the acclaimed screen and stage actor from the early twentieth century, Lon Chaney. He starred in old Hollywood films, such as *London After Midnight*, *The Hunchback of Notre Dame* (which was originally a horror film back in the day), *The Monster* and, of course, *The Phantom of the Opera*. His eclectic performances, paired with his penchant for styling his own wigs and painting his own mug (doing his own make-up), earned him the alias 'the man of a thousand faces', much like me in drag: 'the queen of a thousand faces' . . . or maybe just two faces if you catch me on a sesh. Another thing I have in common with Lon is perfectionism – take from that what you will. This one seemed to have a good ring to it and – *voilà!* – Lawrence Chaney was born. It just sounded like a name you would see in lights, and it stuck with me.

Pick it Yourself . . . Or We'll Do it for You!

I want to take a moment to introduce you to Tallulah von Fuckbucket. There is a lot to be considered when choosing the drag name and it's easy to get wrong. Sometimes you need the wise words of a fellow queen to help avoid disaster. This is why a few of us felt it was necessary to take matters into our own hands when a Dundee queen found herself at a loose end when trying to choose a name.

The person in question was a bit conservative. She disliked swearing, innuendoes and everything in between. Her ideas were a bit dull and might have struggled to make a splash onstage. We thought about it collectively. This girl needed a name and she needed it fast. Enter, Mystika Glamoor. Mystika (a performer from Edinburgh) had just delivered an excellent performance parodying a fortune teller, and had dubbed this poor woman with the name 'Tallulah von Fuckbucket'. Needless to say, it stuck.

It had a French-glamour, old-Hollywood feel, but it was also something that made her squirm. She was of course not a fan of Tallulah von Fuckbucket, but once it was out there, that was that. She has now grown to accept her fate and wears the name with pride. The moral of this story is: pick a name or we'll pick one for you. Or just ask for some advice from your drag sisters. This community is not shy when it comes to creating shady nicknames, so if you'd rather choose your own destiny, pick a name before you step out onto the scene. Alternatively, you are welcome to join the House of Von Fuckbucket.

Keep it Clean-ish

Names like Iva Dong may not allow you to be on prime-time, pre-watershed TV, so if you want to be the next Jackie Bird or HRH Lorraine Kelly, you need to avoid those names. As drag becomes more mainstream, we are opened up to a wider range of career opportunities but there are still those that see this as an 'adult' art form. It is up to you to decide what type of persona you want to give out to the world, but just don't expect to be stepping in for Phil and Holly if you're called Penny Tration.

Keep it in the Family

Some queens share their name with their drag mothers. For any of you that aren't familiar with this term, a drag mother looks out for her drag children, teaching them how to beat their face and helping them come up on the scene. It's a bit like when you're shite at Maths, so your maw forks out for an expensive tutor to try to get you through the year . . . only significantly more stylish.

If you have watched shows like *Pose* (which focuses on New York City's ballroom scene in the late 80s and early 90s), you will see that 'mothering children' was used in a much more literal sense. Traditionally, house mothers (or fathers) would give young queer people somewhere to live and put food on their table, after they were ousted from their homes or abandoned by their biological families.

Today's drag mothering isn't quite as literal as the house mothers or fathers from ballroom. Before this turns into *Rent* the musical, I will clarify that drag mothering nowadays is more commonly just a queen with a bit more experience than you, who will buy you a vodka Red Bull when you're skint. If you are part of a drag family, you've already won half the battle of choosing a name. Think Jaida Essence Hall and Kahmora Hall, or Chad Michaels and Morgan McMichaels. Before you get any ideas, I've got one wean and that's enough for me! I don't want to hear the pitter-patter of any more little Chaney stilettos any time soon.

Find a Middle-aged Muse

Important as it is to try to be original and true to yourself, there are more drag queens than neds in Scotland nowadays, so don't sweat it if you have to brainstorm for a bit before you choose the perfect name. If all else fails, just opt for a random middle-aged woman's name. I've always liked Brenda or Maureen, Mo for short. Anything that sounds like a Glasgow maw who could knock you out.

There is a good formula to it. Think of one of your mum's pals and then ask yourself this. Does she have a bob? Aye? OK, now does she own a Shih Tzu or Bichon Frise? Perfect. Is she the type of person who complains at a restaurant when her food's thirty seconds late? Ideal. Whatever her name is, if she fits that brief, you've got yourself a solid maw drag name.

Don't Get Sued

There is always the option to adopt a famous person's name with a pun. This can either go really well or very badly. (No shade to Fanny Lennox.) Be careful, though, you don't want to end up getting sued. Trust me – if you cannae afford a good lace front, you cannae afford a lawsuit. Avoid names that are too difficult to spell, some people struggle with spelling and pronunciation, you know! (Praise be to my editor.) Oh, and for the love of God, do not call yourself Ru anything. There is already a wee queen aboot called RuPaul Charles.

Drag Name Dos and Don'ts

To save you time, I've compiled a list of things you should avoid and I've even given you a bunch of names you can have for free! Snap them up quick: once they're gone, they're gone. You don't have to take my advice, though, what do I know? I only won *RuPaul's Drag Race UK* . . .

- ✓ **DO** choose a good pun name. (I'll be the judge of this.)
- ✓ **DO** pick a name that's original. There are more drag artists than ever, so if you've come up with a name nobody has used already, take it and run! Even if it's shite, at least it's *your* shite.
- ✓ **DO** name yourself something that can be shortened or easily turned into a nickname. To put it kindly, human brain span isnae quite what it used to be, so if you can keep it short, you're onto a winner.

✔ **DO** reference your idols. (Lorraine Kelly, I'm looking at you, hen.)

✔ **DO** choose a name that will catch on easily. Please note this step will be easier to achieve if RuPaul becomes fond of repeating your name in a terrible Scottish accent.

✘ **DON'T** choose a bad pun name. (Again, I'll be the judge of this.)

✘ **DON'T** choose anything that ends with Divine. Sorry.

✘ **DON'T** go for a name that someone else already has. Do your research . . . It's not that hard to do a wee Facebook or Insta search to see if someone has the name already!

✘ **DON'T** pick a triple-barrelled name. You'll be paying extra when you're making that merch. Ask yourself, do you really need a three-parter?

✘ **DON'T** name yourself anything overtly offensive, it's not worth it, babes. Run it past a few of your hetty pals if it's a bit risqué.

✘ **DON'T** base it on someone you know in real life, unless they give you permission. It'll be awkward when you bump into them and have to act none the wiser.

✘ **DON'T** go for something with complicated spelling. Please don't call yourself Lindsay:

there are simply too many ways to spell that godforsaken name.

The Name Game

To help you along, here's a free-for-all of names. Some are terrible, some are iconic:

* Anita Sidoon
* Gaynor Fewpounds (we've all been there!)
* Anna Glypta
* Amanda Hold (something we all need)
* Mhairi Joanna (I've heard she has a hot box)
* Mary Hill (one for all my north Glasgow queens)
* Sue Namé
* Sue De Crème (good for that chub rub!)
* Shirley Knott
* Anne Widdicunt (for those queens that cannae even straighten their hair)
* Dana Shytte
* Anna Philaxis (what a shocker)
* Barbara Izum (begins at home)
* Gigi Hadidnae (a Scottish supermodel)
* Mia Moré
* Mandy Drip (not pre-watershed friendly)
* Began Thee Stallion (if you're a bit of a beg)
* Lisa Life (my personal fave).

4
Drag 101

If you want to make an impact straight away, you've got to nail your look from head to toe. Having something that makes you uniquely *you*, and therefore memorable, will allow you to stand out from the crowd. As I mentioned earlier, my love of all things purple was inspired by my gran, but there are so many other potential sparks of inspiration to be found – from your personal life to general pop culture. Anything that interests or resonates with you is a great place to start! In this chapter I'll be sharing my hot tips to make sure you're hitting the scene looking like a polished queen and no' a hot mess.

Wiping Front to Back

This drag guide wouldn't be complete without some tips on how to beat yer mug. These are just my personal preferences, so take them or leave them, but they have worked out quite well for me. You'll be shocked to find out I wasnae always this gorgeous. It has taken me years to get to where I am with this art form and like any good make-up artist, when I started out I was . . . shite. One of the most valuable lessons I've learned in life is that you need to get through the bad before you get to the good stuff. It applies to all areas of life. If you think you are going to pick up a brush for the first time and be able to look like your favourite queen, get that idea out of your head. You will fail over and over again each time you try out something new. Practice makes perfect here, so you've got to be patient.

Like any art form, make-up is subjective. Nobody can tell you the 'correct' way to paint your face, as a lot depends on your style and personal preference – but I'm going to try. The options are endless and you can be as creative as you like. If there is any place to really go OTT with the make-up, though, it's through drag. The rules are there to be broken and reinvented, but first you need to know your basics.

Generally speaking, the standard 'drag-queen look' revolves around feminization of the face. This isn't everyone's desired look, and much like drag itself, all make-up is valid – there are no rules. Cover your face with crayons if that's your thing. I won't tell you it looks shite, but the audience might, so it's all up to you if you want to take the risk. I want to give my advice on what works for me, however, if you're going for something different, feel free to skip ahead. Most facial feminization requires everything to be angled upwards: if it's up then it's stuck, as Cardi B would say. Turn that frown upside down, hen.

I'm about to guide you through some of the 'standard' drag make-up routines and give you pointers on what to aim for and avoid if you want to achieve a certain look. Take it from the gal who painted the depression on all because of the shape of my eyebrows for seven episodes; there's a knack to this thing. I've had my ups and downs, so you don't have to! I also would like to recommend some of my personal favourite products. I'll tell you how to use them best and why I use them – sometimes I don't use them for their intended purpose!

YouTube is Your Friend

When I first started practising make-up, there wasn't a whole lot of advice to follow. The YouTuber beauty industry is saturated now and there are a million resources to pull from. You can learn to do virtually any make-up look just by watching a tutorial online. I wish this had been about when I was starting out. It would've saved hunners of bother. Veteran MUAs like NikkieTutorials have been providing us with tips and tricks for as long as I can remember and they're still going strong. Well in, Nikkie hen, may we all be blessed with the career longevity that you have earned.

Even though it was limited, there were still some great tutorials out there on how to do everything from everyday looks to full glam make-up. My expertise lies within drag make-up, but you can use my tips on highlighting and contouring and apply them to non-drag make-up easily too! One of the best bits of advice I can give is to blend, blend, blend . . . and just when you think you're done, blend it some more.

When I started playing around with make-up between 2011 and 2013, there was a massive gap in the market for drag make-up content. That's why so many queens will describe themselves as 'self-taught'. There isnae some magical academy on a secret island to teach us, so we've got to do it ourselves! I remember at first I would use my mum's eyeliner and foundation, but because of how sheer it was, I realized I needed something thicker. That make-up wasn't easily accessible in local shops in 2011, so I moved on to acrylic paint. No, that's not a misprint. Acrylic paint. Funnily enough, I would not advise this these days, but it allowed me to change the colour of my foundation and make it opaquer. Taking the paints I would usually use on canvas helped me map out the all-important shapes of the drag make-up looks I wanted to achieve.

Miss Fame from Season 7 of *Drag Race US* was one of the first to post full drag tutorials online, in late 2013. I put down my acrylics and watched her in awe. Seeing her do her make-up in her own way was fantastic, but she has some beautiful natural features that I haven't been blessed with. All I had been blessed with was a double chin! I didn't want to embrace or enhance any of my natural features, so I had to learn ways to pretend they didn't exist. I used techniques I learned from her to transform the structure of my face.

I owe a lot to queens like Miss Fame, and, who knows, I might've still been drawing my eyebrows on with paint if I hadn't stumbled upon her channel. Can you imagine the state of me, scrubbing that off every night? If only I knew when they said 'paint your face' they didn't mean literally. Can you imagine my dad walking in and seeing me? 'PHYLLIS! Get the white spirit. Lawrence has got the paint out again . . .'

Skincare . . . Straight Men Can (and Should) Do it Too

Before you start, you'll have to get rid of any unwanted facial hair. Shaving is an important part of the prep that's needed beforehand, as even the smallest of hairs can change the texture of your make-up. It's best to go for a full clean-sweep — unless you're like my friend Perry Cyazine and you're a bearded queen. For most of us, our dads didn't teach us how to shave because we were too busy nailing the 'Bad Romance' choreography in our bedrooms, so we had to teach ourselves.

Shaving with the grain is the best way to avoid rashes and irritation, but I would strongly advise feeling over your face afterwards to find some bits where stubble may still be lurking, and shave those against the grain (the opposite direction from which your hair grows). Be careful, you don't want to risk getting any ingrown hairs: they are unsightly wee bastards.

Don't underestimate how much moisturizing the skin helps. Looking after your skin is the first step in any kind of make-up. For all the straight boys out there, or if you've got a man, get them to read the following three words carefully: MOISTURIZE, MOISTUR-IZE, MOISTURIZE. I've heard straight guys saying, 'Skincare is for poofs.' Believe that if you wish, but don't come crying to me when you look like a burst leather couch at the age of thirty. Also, please take note, heterosexual males, washing your face with hand soap and water doesn't count as a skincare routine. Look after your skin, get that sun cream on! (Unless you're in Scotland.)

Using a primer is another great way to prepare your canvas, and most decent primers come with the added benefit of blurring your skin texture and giving your make-up something to stick to. You may need to try out a couple of different primers based on your skin type. Some products are made for dry skin, some for oily and some for combination skin.

PRODUCT RECOMMENDATION

Benefit POREfessional Primer – This product mattifies your whole skin and covers pores, making your face all one even texture. A little goes a long way! This primer is silicone-based (the last time I heard that, I was purchasing something very different . . .) and designed for oily and combination skin to prevent shine breaking through your beat.

The Brows are the Nipples of the Face

One of my favourite details to add in my make-up is matching my brow colour to my wig. You can use a simpler blonde or brown brow for something a little more understated, but I think your face pops so much more when you have a bright purple ombré brow to match that bright purple wig.

Using your natural brows is something that will definitely make colouring a little harder. There are so many tutorials out there on how to cover your brows with glue sticks, but as you might have noticed, more and more drag artists these days choose to shave off a section, or even their entire brow. Don't make the same mistake I made with this, however: if you go all the way and shave the whole thing off, please make sure you know how to draw on a semi-believable out-of-drag brow before stepping outside . . .

If you can't quite part with your forehead facial hair yet, go for the glue-stick method. Glue in circular motions to get complete coverage. If you've got an eyelash or brow comb to flatten them out, perfect. Just don't use a fork and you'll be grand. Brushing through allows you to smooth the whole thing down. We don't want any Weetabix crust.

PRODUCT RECOMMENDATION

iMagic Flash Palette or *(if you're bougie and don't just shop online)* **Make Up For Ever Flash Palette** – A lot of people tend to use brow pomades, which I think are great for the natural look or doing out-of-drag make-up. However, often the colours for brows I go for are quite out there. If you get one of these flash palettes, you immediately have so many colours available to you from just one product. There are coloured pomades available, but I've found the more vibrant they are, the streakier they can get. I like to use these products because the colours are much creamier, more blendable and won't dry up before you finish perfecting that sharp brow.

Holding on to the Cracks in Your Foundation

I've tried every foundation under the sun – sheer, matte, dewy – all by mistake, to be honest. Because my skin is almost translucent, I like to use a base foundation that's one or two shades darker than my natural skin tone before I go in with highlight. This helps the highlighting colour pop more on the face and look more dramatic, like a lovely Neapolitan ice-cream sundae. Pay attention to the undertone of your skin, too. If you have yellow or peachy tones in your complexion, you may be warm toned. Alternatively, if you have pink or blue tones, you may be cool toned. Most good foundations have variants of each shade with different undertones.

The story of how I found my favourite foundation is rather amusing. The baby doll of Dundee herself, big Ellie Diamond, was cutting about the clubs talking about this amazing new foundation she had tried . . . from Primark. Instantaneously, the entirety of the Scottish drag community laughed in unison. Ellie had the last laugh, though. When we actually tried it, well . . . Saying it was life-changing is a total understatement.

Setting powders are something many people seem to think are a myth, instead opting to pile talcum powder onto their wet foundation – myself included. I'm personally no' too snobby about setting powder. However, I will say, either make sure it's translucent or that it matches the colour of the foundation underneath it. Mind how you always hear people talk about beating your mug? Well, you've gotta press that powder on until your face begins to bruise. For maximum efficiency, of course.

PRODUCT RECOMMENDATION

Primark Foundation & Contour Stick – These sticks are £2.50 a pop and will run out a little faster than the average foundation stick. The creamier consistency of the product makes them an absolute dream to blend, without losing coverage. These are excellent for anyone starting out because the price point for the quality is amazing. Don't start off buying expensive products – keep those for the Christmas list.

The Contouring 3: Lanza Made Me Do it

Highlighting and contouring are one of the biggest factors in the perfect drag face. There are endless opinions on what works best. It's also worth noting that a lot of your favourite queens have had a few nips and tucks, so don't compare yourself to something that isn't real. There is a new pandemic in the community (thankfully unrelated to a certain other pandemic), and that is the use of Facetune, an app which allows you to blur, blend and distort your face and add filters. (I'm looking at you, Coco Montrese.) I'm not judging anyone – you do you, babes – but we all have visible lace that we haven't cleaned in three months. Just don't put the pressure on yourself to expect anyone to look like that in reality. Female features tend to be longer and thinner than male ones and that is why you see a lot of elongated and slim nose contour and defined cheekbones.

Where to start with highlighting and contouring, you ask? Well. A prominent brow bone is a typical 'masculine' facial feature, and this is why we contour this area to get rid of the shadows and give a more rounded look. Other target areas for contour are the cheekbones, the sides of your nose, your chin and your jaw. One of the unfortunate ailments that run in my family . . . we were all born wae nae necks. No problem: just draw one back in with your contour brush!

Highlighting under the cheekbones so they are more defined and higher up will also help achieve a more typically feminine facial structure. Focusing the highlight on the centre of the face's high points will bring them forward and create contrast with the shadows. It's critical that you blend like your life depends on it. Sometimes I do like to have a more dramatic look with stark white, thin nose highlights and extra-defined cheekbones that are less blended. You can always take it up a notch, so don't be afraid to play around.

PRODUCT RECOMMENDATION

Kryolan TV Paint Stick, Shade 070 (Clown White) – I've only ever used one product for highlighting. It's tried and tested, and although it's a little more on the expensive side, it'll last for ever. This foundation stick is perfect for getting that crisp, white highlight, and blends into the rest of my base perfectly.

NYX Contour & Highlight Pro Palette – I strictly powder contour these days. Some may disagree; however, I find that on ladies of a slightly larger stature such as myself, powder contouring gives a smoother blend. It lends itself to that 'airbrushed' look, rather than having foundation lines all over your face. This palette has plenty of cool, neutral and warm-toned browns, so you can easily find the colour that best works with your skin tone. I personally like blending them all together!

Read My Lips

Lipstick is something that, much like brows, also never quite gave me the selection I wanted. All the stock in my local shops just . . . don't have the range. I don't really mess with liners, glosses, oils or whatever the kids are using these days. If the product has pigmented colour and stays on all night, that's what matters to me. Sometimes I'll actually find myself using other products, like the aforementioned Flash Palettes, to achieve colours that are hard to find in a purpose-made product (i.e. purple again!!).

Pay attention to the lips and how they would look with varying expressions and positions. Do not draw them too wide. Some queens will spread the lips right on to the cheeks and naturally they will crack, and you will end up looking like The Joker. Practise how your lips look when you are smiling, laughing, frowning, crying your eyes out, etc. Trust me, I know what that's like, I've cried on national television with cracked lipstick and black teeth, and it's not a good look.

Finishing Touches

This is often the part where your make-up goes from serviceable to you becoming the most drop-dead gorgeous goddess diva that's ever put her stilettos (note – character shoes) on the Earth's unworthy soil, yass mawma house down boots the house.

I use a black liner pen to draw on two moles under my eyes and one above my brow. I draw moles to add detail – adding small details like this makes your make-up look like it took ten hours when it probably took you ten minutes.

A lot of people take a set of lashes out of the box and just pop them right on. I think it's really important to customize your lashes – not all lashes will fit your eyes: some may be bigger or smaller. You also may want to stack multiple pairs of lashes on top of each other to give a longer or thicker look. If you're going for a soft and subtle feminine look (like mine), perhaps go for more feathered lashes, not to be confused with actual feather lashes. Trust me. DO NOT. USE. FEATHER. LASHES. NEVER. EVER. EVERRR. Not coloured lashes. Not feathered lashes. If you love yourself, you will NOT. USE. FEATHER. LASHES.

Setting spray is a must. Some still use the old drag trick of setting your face with hairspray, and though this works in a pinch, a purpose-made setting spray will be kinder to your skin and be the final element in destroying any crumbly, cakey textures remaining on your face. (Of course, if you've been following my advice, there won't be many!) While your face is still a little damp from the spray, get any powder highlighter and sparingly apply it to the tip of the nose, the chin, in between the brows and a little on the cheeks. Do not get it in any crevices, and remember, less is more with this step! This one's a bit like *Mission Impossible*, trying to let the setting spray dry enough that the highlighter still blends but not too dry so that it just crumbles off. Putting too much on will ruin all that lovely highlighting and contouring work you've just spent two hours on as well. However, once you find that sweet spot, your cheekbones are visible from Mars. Wae the naked eye. Fact. Ask NASA.

PRODUCT RECOMMENDATION

MAC Cosmetics Dazzleshadow Liquid, Shade 'Diamond Crumbles' – This is my favourite make-up product. Ever. This is funny, because it doesn't do much, but it is glittery and absolutely stunning, with just a hint of purple in it. I use this to highlight my brow bone, despite the intended purpose being a liquid eyeshadow. It's strong, dramatic and bold.

MAC Cosmetics Fix+ Matte – This is my setting spray of choice. I find this keeps my make-up on all night – a good test run was looking at myself next to Ellie Diamond, after a show. The Fix+ kept my make-up stamped to my face, but when I looked over at Ellie I just saw the ghost of an eyebrow that once was. Like the villain from that one movie she likes, her face was melting, meltiiiingg . . . So, I guess we all know what Ellie's getting for her birthday from me.

Threading the Needle

Every single season of *RuPaul's Drag Race* seems to have at least one contestant who quivers at the mere mention of the words 'sewing challenge'. Every single season, the all-important question is raised: why are you coming on to this show if you don't know how to sew? To some extent I agree. I don't care if you can sew or not, but after watching thirteen seasons how can you be shocked when you are asked to sew? A lot of previous contestants have made it work, but an equal amount have seen their demise at the hands of a Singer sewing machine.

The show is a learning curve for most contestants and they always gain some new skills along the way. I say most of them . . . I would advise anyone to have a right good go at it, though. It's not only a skill that'll help you further your career, it will also allow you to give others a helping hand. It might even allow you to develop your own side hustle.

I learned how to sew at the age of eight after I had begged my mum to teach me. I had seen her making cuddly toys for my sister and me, and then, when I was eight, she made me a cape for Halloween. You might think that having my own designer and dress-maker at such a young age would have been good enough for me, but I wanted to learn how to do it myself. I remember the first thing I ever sewed was a squishy version of Krang, from Teenage Mutant Ninja Turtles. I made Krang using an old pillow, a pink T-shirt and some felt for the eyes and mouth. I was so impressed that I could grab some old fabrics and make something brand new.

Front-and-back stuffed plushies didn't hold my attention for too long, and my eyes wandered to more three-dimensional creations. One of my favourite childhood TV shows was *The Avengers* – think less

Chris Hemsworth, more Patrick Macnee. Mrs Peel, specifically, caught my eye. She was a female spy, played by Diana Rigg. Her wardrobe was astounding! (This obsession carried through to adulthood – and even featured on my British Gay Icons runway.) Soon enough, every vest I owned was transformed into a tribute to one of her costumes from the show. The seams were a bit wonky, but listen, I was eight years old! Who was gonna be critiquing my thread tension?

So, whether you can't tell a thimble from a shot glass or you're creating couture with the best of them, here are my tips and tricks for sewing up a storm.

Get a Sewing Machine, Duh!

I would always advise you not to hand sew. A sewing machine will allow you to put together much more complex looks, in half the time. No need to be squinting over your needle and thread in the candlelight! The first ten years of sewing, I had a children's sewing machine that was £20, so there are no excuses, you dogs. I would fire all sorts of fabrics through there. Even if it advised me only to use felt, I had PVC and fur with not a problem.

Once again, online tutorials are your best friend. It's also worth your while to ask around. Can your granny or anyone else you know sew? Have they got a knackered machine that still just about works? Offer to take it off their hands. If you can really nail this skill, you will thank yourself further down the line. It's a very complicated process to create your own garments, so give yourself time to really get to grips with it. If you have skills in pattern-cutting, drawing or basically anything that uses your creative flair, now is a good time to implement them. I would say that it's not for everyone. Just look at Tia Kofi. I look at that girl and the first thing that comes to mind is *God loves a trier*. Tia did the best thing any hapless beginner seamstress could do . . . and paid someone else to do it for her.

Keep it Simple

If you are new to sewing, my number-one top tip is that stretch fabric is a girl's best friend. Cutting a pattern is a whole skill in its own right, but if you use material with a bit of give it'll hide all number of mishaps and dodgy measurements, making it far easier to get away with!

If you are the forty-seven-year-old MILF known as Lawrence Chaney, you will want to work with velvet, floral patterns, or something a bit more mature. There's a whole world of fabric and fancy designs out there, but I strongly suggest you don't overcomplicate what you want to make, especially at this stage.

When you're a sewing novice, set your expectations low. Literally sew something with a front and back, and if you're feeling fancy, two sleeves and a precariously hot-glued bow. That's all it needs for your first foray into sewing a garment. Once you perfect this, you can move on to something else. People get obsessed with working on their stitching, but unless you're working in A&E, no one cares about that. You're doing drag, it's not about meticulous, double-folded hems. It's about throwing fabric through the damn sewing machine and hoping you end up with a nice enough dress for the bingo you're hosting in twenty minutes.

Gather Round

Gathering is a technique where you shorten the length of a material by creating pleats or soft folds. I use this a lot, particularly when making bows and frills, and to add volume around the sleeves and shoulders. It's a very simple way to add more detail and make plain fabric more interesting to the eye. I recommend doing one stitch running down the fabric you would like to be ruffled. Once sewn, start pulling either end of the thread, and the fabric will begin to gather and shrink.

It is relatively easy yet so effective – but does require a little patience. Little details like this appeal to that part of your brain that wonders *Ooh, how's that done?* It can be a bit tricky at first to get your head around, but once you master a few tricks like these you are onto a winner. Then you can move on to stoning the absolute shit out of your garment, until your fingers bleed! Nobody said this was going to be easy!

No H&M

Joe Black – this is your trigger warning . . .

If you can sew, it gives you more freedom to incorporate your own references and ideas. Store-bought stuff is great and has saved my arse many a time, but it doesn't allow you to bring fully realized concepts to life as you don't have full control over the garment.

I love a spending spree as much as the next lady of leisure, so in the past I've had to have a word with myself. Before I fill my online basket up, I say, 'Lawrence, do you *really really* need that? You've got two hunner jumpsuits sprawled across your floor already.' I'd rather fire up the sewing machine and get creative. When you stick to popular retailers and run into a queen with the same outfit on, you can't really say 'bitch stole my look'! On top of that, it's easy to spend more and more money, trying to find something that you like or something that actually fits. The when-you-order-it vs when-it-arrives meme is very real.

If you are at a stage where you want to experiment with different looks but don't want to fork out on the materials, get yourself out to the shops and use your imagination. I've been there many times. Don't forget, a big part of drag is all about taking something old and making it new. Don't be afraid of a charity shop. You can find lots of gems in here without breaking the bank. You might stumble across some old sequinned dresses or a fabulous organza number that a wifey once wore to her estranged sister's wedding. All these things can be brought back to life on the sewing machine, or even with a couple of rhinestones.

Bringing the Body Together

OK, you've sewn your garment and beat your face. What is a stunning costume and pristine beat without a fabulous body to put it on?! It goes without saying that corsets and padding are a personal decision, and you should always do what you're most comfortable with. I personally enjoy adding fifteen-inch hips and an arse that has its own orbit. This is another thing I absolutely love about drag – you can change your silhouette into near enough anything you want. Just use a few bits of foam and a hellish steel-lined contraption that makes your waist reminiscent of a wasp's (known by the locals as a 'corset').

The Bass in the Back

These days, there are quite a few local drag busi-nesses that will make you a wondrous set of pads that will turn your body from nae-ass to hourglass. I would always take a crack at making your own first, though! The jokes about wearing half a sofa on your rear are true – local to me in Glasgow, there is a foam shop. They sell foam for reupholstery, making pil-lows and the like. The first few times I went in to buy foam for pads, I was a little shifty and tried to make excuses: 'Aye, my chair's foam has disintegrated. Again!'

Little did I know, a good chunk of their business actually comes from the Glasgow drag scene!

Now, you've got your big foam blocks. How the hell are these going to become the curvaceous hips that you want so badly? Well, the answer is simple – an electric turkey carver. Stay with me, I promise I'm not talking a crock of absolute shite. This is quite difficult to explain in writing (and I would recommend pulling up a tutorial video), but essentially you need to meas-ure from just above your hip to around halfway down your thigh. Draw a sort of oval shape onto the foam as long as the measurements – don't forget to add a big bump for the dump truck you want to give yourself – then cut it all out with the turkey carver. You could use scissors, but there's a good chance the world will hit another ice age by the time you're done.

Then all that's left to do is smooth out the edges, whack them in seven pairs of tights and you're good to go. Safety first, though! Always cut away from your body and keep your other hand out of the way. Please, please don't accidentally carve your fingers into this year's Christmas centrepiece . . .

Breathe in . . .

Corseting is another special form of torture that many drag artists partake in. To be honest, I think we're aw masochists. When you're first starting out, a generic fashion corset from somewhere like Amazon will be fine. This will help to bring your waist in a little, and if you're wearing padding, corseting helps to smooth things out significantly. After you're in a position to invest a little more into your aesthetic, you might want to look into getting a corset made to your measurements with good steel boning. When you look at artists like Dita Von Teese or Violet Chachki, this is what they've got on. These corsets actually sculpt the shape of your waist – using steel gives them strength and durability like no other.

Legs for Days

The final step in bringing the body together is tights. If you don't want to use pads, you might just want to pop a set of fishnets on your stunning pins and call it a night – just moisturize those knees! However, if you are using padding, you're going to want to get some opaque tights to cover them up and smooth them out. Don't go buying those sheer tights that your aunt wears to work, you're gonna need something a bit more heavy duty. Dance tights are the best direction to go in – they come in a good variety of colours to match your skin tone and they have the elasticity you need to pull the pads flush to your body and leave no bumps! One pair usually doesn't cut it either – I've found that three or four sets are sufficient to smooth everything out perfectly.

The main takeaway from this section should be – you can present your body however you want. These tips are just what works for me, but many people will do it differently. Finding what makes you most comfortable in your own skin on stage is what should be paramount – not conforming to what others may tell you that you absolutely have to do.

Wigging Out

If your goal in drag is to be the next J-Lo, then your buzzcut probably isn't gonna cut it. Unfortunately, wigs are one of the priciest parts of this whole process. I sometimes envy Sasha Velour and Ongina . . . They probably saved themselves a good few grand on hair over the span of their careers. Anyway, let's talk about how to get the most out of your wigs without having to sell your organs.

Purchasing Your First Wig

While you might throw a lot of money on branded make-up that might do the same as a cheaper option, wigs are largely different. Wigs are usually quite a good place to invest a little more. For me, it was the re-usability. I've used the same wigs hundreds of times in different styles and, for the most part, people were none the wiser. If you don't have £200 to sink into a wig, though, don't fret! These days, there are a lot of more affordable options available online – you just need to know what to avoid! Terms like 'costume wig' or – God forbid – 'Halloween wig' are my personal red flags. I wish somebody told me that when I started. In one of my first performances, I performed as Katy Perry in her 'E.T.' music video. Picture it, baby Lawza, in this flat, bright blue, shiny wig. Naw.

Another thing to take into consideration is the hairline on the wig. 'Hard front' wigs generally do not have a hairline and are made with fringes or immovable partings. These are good for some desired looks but can be quite limiting. Lace-front wigs have a layer of skin-toned lace sewn onto the front of the wig, with hairs individually knotted into the lace – giving the illusion of a natural hairline. With these, you can part the wig wherever you want, create up-do styles, French braids . . . They are much more versatile, but that does come with a jump in price point. When purchasing a lace front, make sure the lace is the correct tone for your skin.

Learn to Style

Learning how to style my own wigs was one of the most valuable decisions I ever could have made when starting drag. To be fair, I had a massive head start – my mum was a hairdresser at one point. She really knew her way round a mane. Honestly, is there anything I haven't learned from this woman? She even dusted off her teasing brush when it came to the *Race* and styled some of my wigs! I'm telling you; Phyllis is a living legend.

Your first wig, unless you've sunk about a million pounds into it, is probably going to be made of synthetic hair. Styling these wigs is a little different from when you straightened your hair into absolute oblivion when you were fourteen. Synthetic hair takes better to steaming than the use of heat tools alone – the wet heat moistens the hair and allows the plastic fibres to take on a different shape. Synthetic hair comes in every colour imaginable and a huge variety of lengths.

When getting into styling hair, I strongly recommend purchasing a cork wig block, a stand and some long floral or corsage pins. This lets you secure the wig onto the block and have at it! For the actual styling, you'll also need a wire brush, a teasing brush, rollers and a variety of bobby pins (known as kirby grips here in the UK). Avoid using Velcro rollers – they grip the synthetic hairs and turn your perfectly set curls into a frizzy mess. Trying to figure out roller-set patterns is intimidating, but these days there's a video for everything!

Human-hair wigs are the other hair type available to you. These are significantly more expensive, but they can do a lot of things synthetic hair cannot. While synthetic hair is better for achieving up-dos and massive teased-out curls in a huge variety of colours, it still isn't real hair. If editorial, wet-look hair is what takes your fancy, synthetic isn't going to cut it.

Further to this, human-hair wigs have a way of moving that is just breathtaking to watch on stage – assuming your 'thing' is hairography – and synthetic hair doesn't come close if you're trying to hide the fact you're wearing a wig. You can use a whole manner of heat-styling tools on them effectively and experiment with dyes. Dyeing synthetic hair requires very specific fabric dyes (the hair is made of nylon) and you may end up dyeing the lace hairline of the wig. Unless your skin tone is a lovely bright Shrek green, turning that blonde synthetic wig into a key-lime fantasy might be harder than you think.

Ultimately, it comes down to your budget and

desired aesthetic. If you're learning how to style hair for the first time, I would strongly recommend that you practise on a budget synthetic lace front, rather than your brand-new glossy blonde-Brazilian unit.

Keep Your Hair on!

Every single drag performer has lost their wig on stage at some point. Kudos to you if you haven't . . . but it'll happen to you eventually. It's just a matter of time. All of us have been left snatched in front of a gasping audience at least once, and it's not a good feeling.

One time, I was performing at Acid Betty's show in Glasgow, in AXM. This was back in the early days. Everything was in sepia tone, and I had a lot to prove (or told myself I did). It was one of my first ever support slots for a RuGirl, and I wanted to lift my leg on that stage and piss on it, so to speak. I had my body bound in a PVC dress and I was hitting every (second) beat of 'Pound the Alarm'. Naturally, I was killing it. I decided it was time to diversify from the Ellie Diamond eight-count and show my amazing gymnastic prowess.

The song came to its crescendo and I was going for gold. I leaped up and threw my legs out – it was time for a jump split.

I'd love to tell you that I landed spectacularly, pounded my groin into the floor and rolled into some mind-blowing choreography, but I think we both know that wasn't the case. You're always told to stretch before doing any strenuous activity, and I had most certainly ignored that advice. I landed, and my legs didn't quite split all the way. When mistakes happen on stage, you have to act quickly and decisively to hide them creatively. My first instinct told me to embody ten-year-old Willow Smith and whip my hair back and forth. Bad idea.

I managed to get around three complete hair flips before my lace front flew off my head at breakneck speed, directly into a sea of unsuspecting twinks. That was the record-scratch moment for me. There I was, just like Natalie Imbruglia, lying on the floor, feeling naked and ashamed. The thumping of the track continued while I sat there like a sack of potatoes. As they say, the show must go on, and I pulled myself back up and finished the track with a grin on my face. When I left the stage, I was mortified. Was this what it feels like to get told you're the weakest link, goodbye?

I can laugh about it when I look back at it – I've come to realize that there are multiple moments in every drag artist's career when they look like an absolute tit on stage. It's inevitable, a bit of a rite of passage even. After you make that mistake once, however, generally you'll do whatever it takes so it doesn't happen again. I have a few tips for keeping your hair on. In this chapter, however, I'll only be talking about wigs, not anger management.

A bit like make-up, a bit of prep work is your first step. If you've got short hair, you can pop on a wig cap and pretty much move to the next step. If your hair is longer, then you may want to braid it back before you put the wig cap on, so you're working with the closest thing you can get to a boiled egg. If you've got no hair, you may still want to use a wig cap, so the wig has something to grip on to – but of course it's not essential. No wig cap? No problem! Old tights work like a charm – just maybe trim the legs a bit so you don't have an unsightly beige ponytail. I like to add an extra step and tape the wig cap to my head. Aye, it might hurt a bit, but what's drag if it's comfortable? I don't exactly do a lot of hair-flipping these days, so for me, basic Sellotape works fine. I know drag artists that partake in so much head banging that they're a concussion risk, and they prefer to use something a bit heavier duty, like duct tape or carpet tape. For legal reasons, I accept no liability if you accidentally tear out your hair trying to keep a wig on for a three-minute performance.

For the front of the wig, you're gonna want to use a glue to keep your wig on. I've seen a lot of people use freeze spray or gluing gels, but what's always worked for me is spirit gum. This is a special-effects make-up product, made of alcohol and resin. To apply, paint around where you'd like to place the wig, and give it a couple of seconds to go a little tacky. Then, press the wig down, keeping stray hairs away from the glue. Keep applying pressure to the wig until it starts to dry – you can use a hairdryer set on cool to speed up the process if you'd like. Finally, you'll want to secure the wig to the cap and tape, generally with pins and grips. Try to keep the pins in inconspicuous areas that are covered by the hair. Ensure you pin the back of the wig in – there's nothing that ruins the illusion more than a stray strand of black hair appearing from under your lavender unit every time you spin around. It isnae a good look, hen!

This chapter sure has been a long one. The different skills you can learn while doing drag are very extensive. We are make-up artists, hairdressers and seamstresses all rolled into one. It can be daunting, but don't be afraid to ask for help from other artists or pull up a video! Supporting local drag businesses is always a great option, too – just have a look on social media and you can usually find a wig stylist or costumier in your area!

Don't get caught up with trying to look like a polished professional straight out of the gate – everybody has to start somewhere! If there's anything drag performers are great at, it's giving opinions – but this is a positive. Criticism and critique are one of the fastest ways to home in on specific hurdles and work on jumping over them. Have patience. Glasgow wasn't built in a day, and the superstar inside you won't be either.

Ultimately, you get to decide what works for you.

Put your own spin on everything you do. I salute you for giving it a go in the first place! This outlet should allow us all to feel elegant, stunning and confident. Express yourself, don't repress yourself. (I wonder how many quotes I can borrow from gay icons before I get in trouble. If you are reading this, Madonna, please know I am your faithful servant. One, two, cha-cha-cha.)

5

Being a Local

After overcoming the bullies and going through the rite of passage known as the 'bedroom queen' phase, it was time to venture out onto the drag scene. Bigger cities are often drag hotspots for local shows and touring shows, but do a little digging and you might find somewhere a little closer to home. Your time as a local drag artist is potentially the most formative of all in figuring out who you are as a performer. This is the time when you make mistakes, network with other entertainers and take your first steps as a fledgling wee artist.

Also, for many who don't have their sights set on international stardom, their local scene is where they will call home for the vast majority of the time they will do drag. Establishing your 'tribe' and finding a safe space that accommodates your nearest and dearest is integral to expanding your horizons.

I was fortunate enough to be able to hop on a train to two large cities (Glasgow and Edinburgh) with a few well-established queer venues that many drag artists could call home. More often than not, the people that you might end up calling 'chosen family' are only a Megabus away.

If you have heard my hit single with the United Kingdolls, 'UK, Hun?', you will know that I went from Helensburgh to Edinburgh and made my name in Glasgow City. If you haven't heard it, what are you doing? Stream it now! Each town and city offered a different outlook on drag, and consequently I have had varying experiences in every place. When I was younger, Helensburgh was known for a lot of things: good fish and chips, beautiful seaside views, great pubs, being the home of all of the United Kingdom's nuclear weapons . . . you know, the usual stuff.

In Helensburgh, I didn't have much of an outlet and repressed many facets of my personality. I was obsessed with *Doctor Who*, horror films and Lady Gaga. You can understand why I didn't have many pals. Who shares such a niche set of interests? Can you imagine me trying to relate to the boys in my class at school?

'Oi, Lawrence, are you watching the football at the weekend?'

Mate, unless Pennywise scores a goal using a sonic screwdriver as the crowd chants 'LoveGame', I won't be tuning in.

In my early teens, it dawned on me that if I were to live life to the fullest, it wouldn't be in that town. They say that you can't run away from your problems, but whoever invented that saying obviously didn't mean that you can't literally, physically run away from your problems, because the second I got the chance I was off to the big city.

When Does Dressing-up Become Drag?

It's hard to put into words when I 'officially' started drag. I've been a camp person who has had fun with make-up and dressing-up since I can remember. (Note: I would never usually minimize the art form of drag by referring to it as 'dressing-up', but looking at a young Lawza, I also don't want to besmirch that same art form by calling what I used to do 'drag'.) Trying to pinpoint the exact time frame when I started drag is impossible, because what is drag? What defines its limits? I remember wearing my sister's school dress and my mum's heels around the house when I was five years old. I didn't have any make-up on, but that could've been my first time in drag for all I know. I hope not.

People from the outside world often perceive drag performers as if they turn up at the job centre and say 'I'm actually a drag queen now. I start on Monday.' This isn't what happens: the journey into drag is a long one.

Seriously, though, when do you become a working drag artist? Is it when you get paid a regular income for performing in drag? Is it when people view you as successful and glamorous? Or does the wig and make-up you wear for attending your pal's empty-flat party count as drag?

For one particular house party, I remember cutting up my clear plastic Art folder to recreate Lady Gaga's latex outfit from the 'Telephone' music video – or should I say Gaga's cinematic masterpiece? Halloween is always a great time for us, because when I was younger it was the perfect excuse to dress up as a pop star, movie star or even a monster from *Doctor Who*, without having to explain yourself too much. Any arsy comments could easily be batted away with 'It's Halloween!' Can you imagine me turning up when all the other boys are dressed up as zombies and rappers in a very niche and specific Lady Gaga music-video outfit, saying 'I'm not gay, it's Halloween!'? Cringe. And for those who I know will ask, the outfit is not something worth sharing with the world. It looked terrible, but God loves a trier.

Generally, most people would define their first time in drag as the first time they left the safe threshold of their home in a wig and make-up. (Mind you, in my case, my first time was in a bald cap and a headscarf.) But for the sake of storytelling, I will follow this formula. Please note, any allure of drag is absolutely diminished by the behind-the-scenes of it all. There isn't anything fashionable about a group of six drag queens trying to get a taxi home at 5 a.m.

There will be highs and lows, so whether your drag career started when you were forced to get ready in a disabled toilet (whilst there was a queue of people that actually needed it banging on the door), or when you made it on *Drag Race*, you get to define it.

Getting a Taste

One of the biggest moments in anyone's drag journey is the first time they see a show. I was seventeen when I decided that I wanted to lose my live drag show virginity. My friend from school, Miriam, and I decided to go together. I've mentioned before that she always had crazy-coloured hair and a really unique look. She'd also shaved her brows off and did these Joe Black high, thin, theatrical eyebrows. So, as you can tell, she was pretty much a drag queen in herself and therefore the ideal person to attend my first ever show with.

We had both turned eighteen the same week and began planning our birthday celebrations. We were huge fans of *RuPaul's Drag Race* and always watched it together. We would spend most weekends just watching highlights reels and some of the queens' live performances online. We'd always assumed that the *RuPaul's Drag Race* tours and live performances had only ever taken place in America, so you can imagine our reaction when we saw an advert for a queens' UK tour. I couldn't believe it. These queens that were a million miles away were going to be in Glasgow, less than an hour away from us. We spotted that one of the season winners was doing a show in Glasgow on Halloween. This was fate. We were going to be able to see a RuGirl perform on our favourite night of the year, to celebrate our eighteenth birthdays!?

It felt quite fitting that it was on Halloween because the show was spooky as fuck. When I set foot in the club and smelled that dry ice, I knew this was the place for me. As I walked through into the main room, I could literally hear my shoes pulling off the sticky floor. Shoutout to AXM: I'm glad you got a refurb.

We walked into the venue, and gazed upon two drag queens checking tickets for the event. This was the first time I'd seen any drag queens in real life. One of them still had a beard. It was so fascinating because I hadn't seen this type of drag before. It really opened me up to what drag could mean. I was used to thinking drag meant you had to be a young, pretty, female impersonator and this was my first exposure to something different.

Perry Cyazine and October Fist were the names of the queens on the door. Seeing drag make-up in real life that wasn't studio lit with the hazy Season 1 *Drag Race* filter was amazing. I finally had the chance to see drag queens in their habitat. It was like going to the zoo where the monkeys throw their shit at you, but instead of monkeys and shit it's drag queens with shot glasses. The now-familiar smell of smoke and alcohol in the air, mixed with the damp heat of sweaty bodies in a nightclub was an assault on the senses back then.

Before the main act arrived on stage, there was a trio of local Scottish queens performing the opening act. RuJazzle, Lacy Rain and one of the queens from the door, October Fist. They did a group performance of 'Applause' by Lady Gaga. It was so fun to hear a song by a musician that you adore being sung by every member of the crowd whilst these queens were killing it on stage and living their best life. What an amazing thing to observe.

The main act arrived and put on a bone-chilling show. It was crazy to see someone you'd only ever watched on television right in front of you. She performed a flawless routine, even singing live, which blew my mind.

Singing was a skill I never possessed. When people say 'anyone can be taught to sing', babes, try me. If any singing coaches are reading this, help a gal out. I want the Honest Vocal Coach to try and reform this croaky bitch. Seeing this show, live and in person, was what made me think: *I'm going to be on that stage one day.* I am not a *Vogue* cover girl. I'm a performer. Hearing the crowd scream and applaud her was something I was desperate to experience for myself.

Through the night people were coming up to Miriam and complimenting her outfit and make-up. A fellow queer person from our school came up and chatted to Miriam, but completely didn't acknowledge me. We were all in the same year at school, we all knew each other, but suddenly he wanted to be friends with Miriam because she looked amazing. When this guy didn't say a word to me, along with many of the other people throughout the night who complimented my friend, I decided that I didn't want to be overlooked any more. I wanted people to feel compelled to come up and talk to me. I wanted to feel that buzz of being the one that everyone was complimenting and looking at.

I had decided there and then that the next show I went to, however far in the future it was, I would go in full drag.

'Siezures' (sp?)

The opportunity for my first outing came around fast. It was December 2014. Jinkx Monsoon and Major Scales were coming to Glasgow, and I was ecstatic. I wanted to pay homage to Jinkx's hilarious 'Snatch Game' impression of Little Edie from *Grey Gardens*. I wore my gran's old fur coat, my mum's scarf and a Smiffys bald cap. It was a sight to behold. I don't think I looked too awful, but you can judge for yourself. Everyone's first time is generally a bit rough. At least, it was back then anyway. Out of drag, I wasn't looked at once. In drag, I couldn't stop people from looking at me. I felt really self-conscious because the taxi dropped me off round the corner from the club and I was scared

I was gonna get shivved. Thankfully there were no granny bashers there that night.

Once I was in the club, everyone was asking me what my name was. For the first time ever, I whispered 'Lawrence Chaney'. I decided it would be interchangeable with my real name and saying it out loud solidified this. I think I stood out because I was dressed like a granny and spoke like a wee Scottish wummin. It wasn't typical of a drag queen to greet someone with 'Awryt, ya bawbag'. I could tell that people were confused and thinking *Why are you talking like that?*

I think my chosen vernacular was jarring to some people, as they were used to the general 'Yass, queen! Slay, hunty!' language.

It was an entirely different experience, seeing the show in drag. At the meet and greet, Jinkx was so kind to me. It was the perfect validation for a budding new queen – she chatted away to me and gave me lots of compliments. Meeting famous drag artists can sometimes be a hit or a miss. Often, these people are touring with at least twenty dates a leg, back to back, meeting over 100, 200 people at each show. I wouldnae blame some poor cunt for no' being at their perkiest at 3 a.m. on the fifteenth consecutive night of their nationwide tour. They aren't machines. You also have no idea what is going on in their life at that time: they could be putting on a brave face whilst going through some tough shit. Just be kind, respectful and patient. It's so fun to get to see people you adore in the flesh, so be friendly and express your feelings, just don't ask them to sign your douche!

My Jinkx make-up look marked the start of a long line of impersonation looks. I started becoming known for coming to the shows dressed as the queen headlining. I painted Trixie onto a fishtail gown. I recreated BenDeLaCreme's snow-leopard dress, hat and all. Then it was onto Alaska, with her signature rat's-nest wig. Pearl's papier-mâché beard. Max's grey glamour. Katya's Baberaham Lincoln. Adore's roller-set look. Manila's tusk dress. Creating looks inspired by these queens helped me throw myself into sewing and improve, try new silhouettes and concepts, and ultimately ended up forming the Chaney you see today!

We're No' in Cardross Any More

A big part of embracing who Lawrence Chaney really is came through networking and connecting with local performers. Finding my 'tribe', if you like. I think that's why *The Wizard of Oz* resonates with so many queer people, as it's actually shown itself to be a great metaphor for the queer experience. You have to go far away from your comfort zone in order to find that you already possess what you sought out in the world. Let's be real, Glasgow isn't quite the Emerald City, but trust me, I've seen some scarecrows along the way.

Scottish drag seemed really unique in a way. Everyone had their own niches. Some wanted to be sexy and fierce, some dark and mysterious, some crazy and kooky and some just downright grotesque. The creativity in Scotland is truly insane, and we have so many diverse styles of drag up here. A big way that I networked was bringing along my camera to gigs. I'd take photos of the performers and tag them online, and this is how we found each other on social media. It was a great way to worm my way into everyone's consciousness, as it were.

Some of my first performances were a bit . . . shaky. My first show was Lacy Rain's Tea Party. Officially, my first ever performance was 'E.T.' by Katy Perry, but I'd been doing jazz hands from when I popped out of my mum's womb. Keep in mind there was a full Kanye West verse on this. You know I kept it in. How could I take it out? The second track I selected was 'Venus' by Lady Gaga. I thought it would be clever to go from my spooky, bright blue 'E.T.' make-up into the particularly feminine vibe of 'Venus'. Boy, did I regret that when I was wiping off my blue face and re-gluing my eyebrows, all in a tiny bar dressing room. It was just awful. I downed a Venom and powered through, as one must, and papped on the seashell bikini and garden panty. Never again.

A quick tangent, just for a minute. I don't think you can talk about the Scottish drag scene without discussing Venoms. This is a Scottish cocktail that you have to try at least once in your lifetime. These things might be absolutely lethal, but they're very much the backbone of Scotland. Venoms are an acid-green drink that must only be served in a pint glass. You need a shot of vodka, a shot of Southern Comfort, a Blue WKD and some orange juice. I would recommend everyone to try this before they die. You'll thank me later.

It was clear I had no identity quite yet. I had gone from impersonating *Drag Race* alumni to pop artists. Like I thought, *Nae pressure, I'll just go emulate Gaga.*

I still didn't know who Lawrence Chaney was as a character. I didn't know my silhouette, I hadn't quite found what make-up worked for me, so instead I lived through these characters and they helped me along the way.

My next show was a fundraiser show – one of my friends had been caught in an unfortunate fire and had lost so much, so we were raising money to get her back on her feet. I chose to take inspiration from Disney and perform as the Evil Queen. I had a transition planned for when I would transform into the old hag. OK, stay with me. Mind how the Huntsman couldn't bring himself to kill Snow White and so he put a pig's heart in the Evil Queen's box instead? Well, I thought the best way to represent this was . . . 'Swine'. By Gaga. I honestly thought I was so clever, but the blank looks from the audience while they tried to figure out what was going on were very telling. I had the building blocks, but I hadn't quite built a tower just yet.

I remember my third show quite vividly as well. Going back to pop icons, I cut up my old school trousers to create matador shorts for a performance of 'Living for Love' by Madonna. I didn't intend the performance to be quite as much of a replica as it ended up being. I walked out in the biggest platform stilettos, stoned for the gods. My foot came flying right back out of the shoe and I hit the floor in true Madge style. I wasn't quite Living for Love; I was more semi-Living for Love. Mainly because I was dying.

Falling Down the Rabbit Hole

Venturing out into the world of nightlife can be scary, especially for those of us (like myself) who launched ourselves into that life the moment we turned eighteen. You end up spending a lot of your time in greasy dive bars where those that have perhaps had a wee bit too much to drink are giving blowjobs in the back alley beside the bins. Silly fuckers. If I were them, I would focus my efforts on raiding the bins, looking for leftover pizza. If you avert your gaze from this, however, the world of nightlife and local drag is truly magical.

Many that partake in drag these days choose to do so as a hobby, a bit of fun on the side while they focus on a different life path. For some, however, they know it's what they want to do for the rest of their life. One of the first people I ever met from my local community was an Edinburgh-based performer named Alice Rabbit. Alice allowed me to take a gaze through the looking glass at what would eventually become my calling – seeing her was what made me slip down the rabbit hole, into the world of smoke, mirrors and performance.

I first met Alice in February 2015 in AXM, at a competition she was participating in. I could have looked at her for hours – she had on a bright blue blazer with a massive tulle skirt, performing an Alice in Wonderland mix. It was so inspiring, seeing someone plus-size tear up the stage the way she does. We got to talking, and she told me of her pipe dream of having a show called 'The Rabbit Hole'.

Alice and I have had quite the variety of bonding experiences. One particularly strange encounter was outside AXM, after the AAA Girls show. I promise you, this is a true story, every last bit. We were waiting outside the club for a taxi at 3 a.m. – no Ubers in 2015, remember? How did we survive?! Anyway, there was this guy standing over in the corner, holding a pizza box. Just . . . holding it. Not scoffing the pizza inside like we would have done, just holding it. This was sign number one that something was afoot.

As time went on and more people dispersed, we were soon standing there alone with him. He began to flirt with us, asking to take us home and saying we both looked beautiful. The pizza box snapped open, and he only had his fully erect penis laying inside. Did this guy come straight out of an early 2000s porno? This cunt must have had his erect dick in this box for what must have been over an hour. How the fuck had that man not taken a stroke, holding all that blood in his cock the whole time? Security didn't really do anything other than chuckle and leave. Alice swiped at the box, closing it, and we were saved by the taxi pulling up. We sat down in the backseats in total disbelief. Alice turned to me. 'That's why you always leave in twos.'

The Royal Mile

Anyway, speaking of Alice. That bitch sure does get shit done, because in September of that year, in CC Blooms in Edinburgh, the first 'Rabbit Hole' show went ahead. I was one of the first to fall down the rabbit hole, as it were, performing as Margaret Thatcher singing over 'Bitch Better Have My Money' by Rihanna, and 'Poker Face'. (Incidentally, I altered 'Poker Face' so that it was 'Tory Face – We're going to spend your money'.) The pinnacle of my career, I think. Performing as Margaret ironically was the first big elevation forward in my drag – more styled hair, a better-fitting outfit, and an evolution in comedy. Alice's show was one of the first weekly shows in Scotland with a cast of residents, and really set a precedent.

I managed to win Alice over with those numbers, and she said she'd love to book me more. I started to come and support the show on weeks I wasn't performing, bringing my camera along and getting snaps of the show as well as some videos of the performances. There's no bigger struggle when trying to get a show off the ground than facing the challenge of getting promotional material prepared and out there as quick as possible. I wanted to help in any way that I could. Our personal relationship grew, which ended up growing our professional relationship too.

Alice put me on the roster of residents, which opened up many doors for me. I had somewhere regular to test-run funny mixes, sexy performances, straight tracks and a bit of mic work here and there while Alice got changed (or was too inebriated to put a sentence together).

Edinburgh really started to take off for me. I would meet other artists from Edinburgh, Glasgow and Dundee when they came to perform guest spots at the Rabbit Hole, and it all expanded from there. I got to know Jon Pleased Wimmin, a notorious drag DJ who rose to fame in the 90s. He had a show just upstairs in the main bar, called 'Church of High Kicks', and I began to perform there regularly alongside the Rabbit Hole. Groundskeeper Fanny, another

Rabbit Hole resident at the time, had me as a resident at her monthly cabaret show in Electric Circus, near Waverley Station – 'Such A Drag'.

This is ultimately why in 'UK, Hun?' I said, 'From Helensburgh to Edinburgh.'

Every week, I was skinting myself and paying over thirty quid to get to the capital and back, just to perform. I started patching college as well – I was so focused on networking, meeting new people and advancing my drag that college started to fall behind. Stagnant. I wasn't learning about comedy in college, it was the classics, like *Othello*. My lecturers could see this distance happening and said they wouldn't blame me if I dropped out. I continued, though. I wanted to at least finish the year.

While Edinburgh was working out like a dream to begin with, things began to get difficult as time went on. The longer you seem to spend doing drag, more and more often, the more political it seems to get, and dangerous. People start shouting at you on the train, or when you're walking the two metres from the taxi to the club. On top of that, relationships with others become more strained, and if you fall out with one person, you run the risk of everyone following suit.

One queen asked me for honest make-up advice. I'm not sure what she was hoping for, but honest advice it was not. I suggested that she could maybe change the shape of her brows – they were a bit crooked and resembled the McDonald's arches. Mind you, I probably could have worded it a bit better, but I was trying to be truthful like she asked! That and I'd had a few drinks. She later turned and said to all her friends that I had flat-out called her make-up shit. The situation snowballed and started to catch up. You've really gotta be careful of the things you say, especially while under the influence, cuz they can come back and sink their teeth into your padded arse.

The Godmother

On a lighter note, another amusing story from my times in Edinburgh comes to mind. Roché Rabbit, one of Alice's drag daughters and a real-life cousin, had departed from a show one night with a gentleman caller. This was a problem, as Roché also happened to own the flat we were meant to be staying in that night. Alice was stood outside CC's at the end of the night, no wig, no wig cap, sliders and a green fringe dress. We managed to just about find her, at the bottom of a mammoth flight of stairs that go round the back of the venue and beyond.

'Roché! We're meant to be staying at yours the night! Where are you going?!'

Where were we gonna go? There were no hotels accepting walk-ins at that time of night, not that it mattered because we were absolutely penniless.

Alice was furious, hollering down the alley of steps.

It was a bit like if Marlon Brando in *The Godfather* was actually a bald, Scottish flapper.

'Hawl! You're done! You're over!'

Roché was out of range, however, and we lost sight of her. I started to panic a little, because by this point my phone had died. We started to trudge along to the nearest McDonald's, in the hope of a plug point to charge my phone and a few chicken nuggets to soothe our emotions.

We started to approach the McDonald's, Alice dragging her suitcase behind her. She had been incredibly busy at the time, travelling constantly, and was practically living out of that suitcase. It was beaten and abused, missing a wheel, and very much looking like it was ready to pass to the other side. I began to calm down as we got closer to the warm glow of McDonald's, and . . . the door didn't open. They were closed. For refurb. At 4 a.m.

Well, that was that. I went into overdrive, freaking out. It was 'Rats: the Rusical' before 'Rats: the Rusical' even happened. My parents had no idea where I was, I barely had an idea where I was. Alice also went into overdrive, but it was one of fury, not hysteria. We were both drunk, and neither of us could remember Roché's address. Alice started fumbling around again, absolutely raving that she couldn't find her card. She said she checked everywhere. It was the straw that broke the camel's back. She lifted the suitcase by the extended handle, drew it back and, like a golf swing, slammed it into the McDonald's window.

A hole in one it was not. Those windows must be made of some Area 51 shit, because they're bloody immovable. Alice flew backwards and fell flat on her arse. The case did absolutely nothing. Something glittered, catching my eye as it flew out of an open pocket on the front of the case. Alice's card. Quite gracefully and poetically, everything was in slow motion as it made a perfect arc out of the case and down a drain. Alice, none the wiser, began unzipping her suitcase again, still looking for it.

'Alice. Alice. It's down the drain, Alice. It just fell down the drain.'

We continued our walk down Princes Street, past a multitude of closed shops. These were the days that I like to refer to as BNM. Before the Night Megabus. Dark, dark times for performers everywhere. I stared at my dead phone, starting to think we were both probably going to end up dead. It was lucky that the street was quiet, because the most Alice could've done in that dress was offered to rotate on the spot and wash an assailant's car.

Eventually, we arrived at the McDonald's on the other side of Edinburgh. It's not really on the other side, but it felt like that. I plugged my phone in, and texts from Roché popped up. Apparently, she had come to her senses.

'Where are you? Will I come and meet you?'

We had left CC's at 4 a.m., it was now 7 a.m. Upon reaching Roché's flat, Alice was no longer the Don. Alice was . . . asleep. I only managed to grab a couple of hours before having to wake up and return to Glasgow for college. They could tell I was dead inside when I turned up. They knew I should have just dropped out, but I couldn't! Ken the student loans?!

Living this duality of a life was literally like night and day. Drag at night, and college by day. I couldn't keep doing both for much longer. Thankfully, I barely scraped a pass on my HNC. Whilst everyone prepared to move on to their diplomas, I focused on drag for the whole summer of 2016.

People Make Glasgow

I began to move my scope back to Glasgow. I scored a residency with Trigger, AXM's weekly drag show. After leaving college, I had no student loan to fall back on and I couldn't just live off my parents, so I had to do the unspeakable – get a job. I started working in Remnant Kings fabric shop in September 2016. Working here helped me to put away a bit of money to pay for fabric and wigs, and I began to get stuck into doing drag more regularly. I could work a 9 to 5, then jump to a friend's house to get ready for the show.

Performing with Trigger was short-lived, and our relationship ended a few months later in December. I dived into the local conceptual show, 'Mothertucker'. My performances got wackier as I brought characters like Zurg and Mr Burns to life. 'Mothertucker' had a more commercial sister show, 'Suck', and I began to get booked there more and more regularly.

Working constantly was a major boost to my self-discovery. I now had plenty of opportunities to prove my worth in Glasgow and figure out what worked for what. While gathered gowns and big coats were great for photos, they weren't as great for performing in – leotards were where it was at. I think every artist has their leotard phase. It's just another one of the rites of passage in drag. I was able to figure out my bread and butter with performing, finding the sweet spot between doing whatever the hell I liked and what the audience wanted to watch.

I had garnered a bit of a following on social media, and I decided to start making online make-up tutorials. This was a nice full circle for me – I had learned how to do make-up by watching Miss Fame online, and now I was in a place where I could impart my own knowledge to others and give back.

In October 2017, I began creating content for BBC the Social. This is the BBC's digital platform, based in Glasgow, that helps to kickstart and develop new talent from all over. It started with a video explaining what drag meant to me at that time, but this quickly developed into a make-up tutorial. Over the following months, I would transform into a *femme fatale*, a Pop

Art zombie, and even Mrs Brown. From there, I took it into the realm of make-up challenges – trying to do a face with only five products and trying out weird trends like fishtail brows. I got to do a couple of comedy sketches, and some more serious videos, like visiting Westminster and discussing why there are no straight Pride events.

These videos were a huge springboard for me. I loved hosting, both videos and being on the mic. I searched for more hosting opportunities, and in February 2018 I became a resident of 'Mothertucker'. I could prepare hosting segments and figure out what I wanted to say, as this was more formal than the stand-in hosting I had done before. I got used to performing a different concept in the show every week. My first night as a 'Mothertucker' resident was the night I was scouted for a documentary about drag in Glasgow. I didn't even need to think about it. I accepted immediately. *Mother Tuckers: Drag Queens of Glasgow*. Right place, right time!

Other than the debut of my dirty tights and cloven hooves, my part on this documentary followed the pursuit of stand-up comedy and the mainstream. (If only someone could have told me where I'd be now!) I spoke about a lot of things that I've now elaborated on in this book: the bullies, how onlookers see you in the street and drag dripping into the mainstream world.

'Even if I don't make it next year, or the year after,

I think I will always be out to put myself out there and make a name for myself.'

Well, babes, the proof is in the pudding! Please remind me to never try and explain tucking to a straight audience ever again . . .

Giving Birth

Birthing a drag child was something that I never really considered. Since I moved from show to show, city to city, constantly working, I don't think the possibility of taking a new queen and showing them the ropes was feasible to me. Not only that, but I felt as if I was someone rather different from many others, with my sense of humour and my totally self-sewn wardrobe. My future daughter came out of nowhere, and I knew immediately I had to take her under my wing.

Paris Ettamol (briefly called Ivy Profen) had come into my workplace to buy some fabric. Listen, I would normally advise you not to name yourself after a pharmaceutical, but it's OK because it's mah wean! Do what I say, no' what I do! She was looking for a white crepe georgette. This raised my eyebrow – this fabric is exclusively used for dressmaking, and very rarely is it applied to anything else. I asked what she was going to make, and she replied, 'Oh, I'm making a robe to perform as the Countess.'

Gaga?! *American Horror Story*?! The relationship immediately flourished.

She had entered one of Trigger's yearly competitions, the Monster Tuck Rally. I went along with some friends to watch, and something about her stuck in my head. She makes her own outfits; I make my own outfits. She leans more into narrative-based performances; I lean more into narrative-based performances. I became a little obsessed. Am I a weird psycho for that? I don't think so. It's rare to see someone quite as similar to yourself sometimes.

The week after, I was unable to attend the show. I was confused why I kept getting tagged in videos from the club. I clicked on a few of them. There Paris was, in a grand Mary, Queen of Scots costume, gliding across the stage. She pulled out a frame, which had a picture of Elizabeth the First inside. Wait. It was me! Me, as Elizabeth the First! Paris had taken the photo of me and cut out the mouth to create a mini paper puppet to use in her performance. I thought it was genius. Now, how do you go about adopting . . .

I stopped in my tracks. I had gotten away with myself a little, and totally forgotten that Paris already had a drag mother. How does one poach a drag wean? Do you offer them a camel in exchange? Paris and I started hanging out more together, and I put the motion forward that I would like to adopt her but didn't know if I could do it. It didn't feel right, it had to come from her – even though she was quite shy and reserved. It's a bit like how your parents cannae ghostwrite your UCAS application. Except UCAS is for the straights, and telling your drag mother that you're running away to the Haus of Chaney is the gay version.

The transfer went rather painlessly. From then on, we were unstoppable. We created looks together, performances – it felt correct that we brought together our separate Mary and Elizabeth acts into a duet, *Kill Bill* style. During all of this, Paris had won the competition and become a Trigger resident. I do hope that a Mothertucker and a Trigger resident coming together in this way perhaps helped to heal a little of the divide between the two shows.

Glasgow Drag Awards

Jumping forward to early 2020, I had received The Call in February. I immediately pulled out of every gig, every stand-up try-out, every pilot and residency, using a couple of predetermined excuses. (Don't worry, I'll give you some suggestions later!) The one thing I had to go to was the first ever Glasgow Drag Awards.

It's like the BAFTAs, but much smaller, and the carpet is pink, not red. The categories had gone out to the local community weeks prior, and the audience and fellow drag artists could vote for who they thought was most deserving of recognition. The nominations were in, and I ended up being selected for four different categories, for which I was immensely grateful.

Kiko, my flatmate, had also been nominated, and Paris had been invited to perform with Kiko and another Trigger resident, Marla Sinner, representing the entire Trigger collective. Paris, Kiko and I all got ready together, and arrived on the pink carpet.

Let me tell you, I had never seen Delmonicas so packed. Delmonicas is an LGBTQ+ bar, located in the Merchant City in Glasgow, and it definitely was not meant to have quite as many people in it as it did that night. We had to shuffle our way through the audience members to get to the stage, and after a little wiggling, we made it. Each category came up one by one, and I ended up snatching both 'Best Comedy Performer 2020' and 'Shadiest Queen 2020'. I find that quite amusing, considering that was the end of February, and a month later I would win 'Leader of Lording It Up' at *Drag Race*. Hey, what's drag without a little shade?

Although my days as a local drag queen are behind me, I do want to return to the local scene in Glasgow and make real change. As I said on the show, I want to improve working conditions for the local entertainers. Is the best way to do that through starting a union, perhaps? Another dream of mine is to open my own drag bar, for drag artists, by drag artists. Maybe one day I'll be able to reach these aspirations. Until then, I will look back on my local community with a great fondness, and always remember the times I've had. I am consistently impressed by the talent and creativity of both the drag artists that I grew up with and each new generation that pops up afterwards. I can't wait to see where Scottish drag goes next.

6

Why is it So Hard? And Why is He Not?

You would think that one's job and one's love life don't really have anything to do with each other. Well, when you're doing drag, this is not the case. For some strange reason, it has an effect on everything. Now, I'm not claiming to be an expert in the dating field, but on multiple occasions I have tried and failed to find love. I'm yet to find the one to sweep me off my hooves – but trust me, this isn't for a lack of effort! There are layers to this thing, much like an onion. I believe it was actually Scottish poet Carol Ann Duffy that first made this comparison, and my God, it rings true (haha . . . like onion rings . . . get it?).

Dating when you are queer can be rocky in any one city, because usually the sample pool of potential suitors is a lot smaller than the selection available to heterosexuals. A recurring theme seems to be that you're probably going to know someone that's shagged anyone you set your eyes on. Being plus-size adds another layer to this whole palaver. Yes, that's right, if you're a fat queer drag queen, you actually need to sit down and write a 5,000-page essay on why you deserve to be loved in today's society before you even get to smell a first date.

Sorry to disappoint, but I can't tell you how to get the man of your dreams. I am simply not qualified to do so. What I can do, however, is tell you about my tragic dating *faux pas*, some major red flags that may end up waving in your face and what socks *not* to wear to your first time out in a lovely restaurant. Fuck's sake, I really should have called this book 'How *Not* to Live Your Life'. Nevertheless, it's time to take my dating corset aff, so to speak, and let it all hang out.

The First Victim

I started dating my first ever boyfriend at the age of eighteen. The first victim, you might say. As I mentioned before, this was the boyfriend that gave me the reason I needed to come out to my family. When you think about that, it's a bit of a shame that it ended with me crying my eyes out a few months later, on my birthday of all days!

He was a dancer. Fit, athletic and tall, i.e. all of the things I am not. Even when I was skinnier, I still felt fat – which is a crazy little thing called body dysmorphia, babes! I'll touch more on that later, don't worry!

Anyway, I met him at Lady Gaga's ArtRave concert. This was still my bowl-cut era, so it's a wonder how he accepted my Snapchat friend request. Mind you, he never did speak to me until I got a haircut . . . One thing led to another, and we set up a date.

When that fateful day arrived, we met up and our relationship blossomed. Please keep in mind that a month for queer people is like three years in straight years, so it was pretty good going!

As the days passed, it was clear that I felt less than the person I was dating. I constantly felt like I was punching above my class, totally out of my league, so it's clear why my self-esteem took such a battering. Getting into this mindset is really dangerous because the insecurities project themselves on to others and find brand-new ways to ruin your relationships with everyone you know. It makes you possessive, jealous and vulnerable. I became a crazy bitch. Putting all your worth into this one person, then becoming so scared of losing them because you don't feel good enough for them is a slippery slope.

Despite my efforts to try and shake off that headspace, finding any evidence that 'proves' the thoughts playing in your head shatters any attempt at positivity. 'Evidence' is a strong word as well, because the reality of the matter is, your brain ends up taking suspicion as fact.

On one of our days out together, we visited the National Museum of Scotland in Edinburgh. It was a brilliant day to begin with – it was nice spending time with him, having a gander around the capital, and gawking at the exhibits in the museum – and then we bumped into one of his male college friends. He seemed lovely at first and greeted both of us. They spoke for the most part as we hadn't met yet, so I was a bit more reserved. The friend later departed, saying how good it was to meet me and that he would see me around soon.

Soon after this, while we were surveying a particularly impressive gown once owned by Mary, Queen of Scots, my boyfriend's phone went off and he flipped it over immediately. Let me tell you, if someone flips their phone over when they get a notification, it feels like an act of war. The simple act flooded my head with doubt, especially since I was already such an insecure person. Are they texting someone else? Are they cheating on me? The paranoia hits hard. It suggested he was being secretive. What did he have to hide? What didn't he want me to see?

I asked him who was texting him, but he brushed it off. I of course grew more insecure and eventually he told me that his friend had texted him. He allowed me to read the message and his friend had stated, 'Why are you with Lawrence? I'm much better looking than him . . . You could do a lot better.'

I then realized that he was actually trying to protect my feelings by not showing me that message. It's one of those moments when you go 'Aww, fuck, I look like an arsehole.' I had totally got the wrong idea. I really admired that he stuck up for me to his supposed friend and called them out for saying something so judgemental.

The 'Break'(-up)

As time went on, instances like this became more common, but during this time I'd built up a strong connection with his family. I've always had an affinity with my boyfriends' mothers, and this particular one was a bit of a legend. I got on with her so well.

One day, it became obvious that the honeymoon period was over and there wasn't as much joy in the relationship as before. I asked him outright if he was only with me because I slotted in so well with his family, and that question derailed the whole relationship. It was his lightbulb moment. He was into me because I made his mum happy – to her, he finally had a nice, caring boyfriend who didn't cheat. Perhaps the connection to each other wasn't quite as strong as we'd originally thought. He suggested that we should go on a 'break'. That fateful word. I hope this word fills you with dread, because unless you've been going out for a significant period of time, we all know what it means.

It was an awful break – aren't they always? He felt like shit; I felt like shit; his mum was devastated, bless her. I went back home and got some brutal advice from my big sister. 'You've only been dating for six months, you don't need a break – what he means is that you need to break up.' Despite the fact it was my birthday, I called my boyfriend and he confirmed he wanted to break up. Damn. I was really hoping my sister had got it all wrong. We properly called it off once and for all.

Take note – as soon as you dump someone, get rid of any expectation of being friends. You need to let yourself feel what you're feeling. Let it all out and only then can you see if there can be a friendship. I realized that I wanted honesty more than anything else in a person. I'm upfront and straight to the point, so I want someone who is the same. Saying that, I'm the sort of person who will be like 'If someone ignores me on Grindr, just say I'm not your type', but when they tell me I'm not their type am like 'You evil nasty fat-phobic bitch'. Drag performers are hypocrites. What can I say?

When you've just been dumped on your birthday, I do think it's out of order to say, 'I don't want to be your boyfriend but I think we can be friends.' I don't want to be your friend. I was so bitter at the time, and hell knows no fury like a drag queen scorned. Like I said, I need people to be straight to the point, but like, not on my bloody birthday!

I now see how I acted wasn't the right way to go about things. I later heard that my ex wanted to start drag too. Cue more psycho-ex behaviour. The first thing I did was go straight to Alice Rabbit (she essentially ran the scene in Edinburgh at the time) and pleaded with her to never book him at a show I was at. I wanted to keep the distance between us and avoid him as much as physically possible.

Handling a break-up is fucking difficult, never mind trying to handle your first one. You go through a million and one coping mechanisms to try and scrape yourself up and on to the next chapter of your life. Continuing with my totally rational decisions, next I decided not to eat. I lost lots of weight in order to be what I thought would be more desirable. I would make drag performances aimed specifically at him, trying to perform out the pain I was experiencing. I was jumping from method to method, never really stopping to actually consider my own emotions at play. What we need to understand is our own emotions and boundaries. Can you be friends with someone who was inside you two days ago? I don't think so. You need to build it up from scratch again, and that takes time.

Years passed without contact, and I don't hold any grudges. I'll talk more about this later, but I think negative experiences can be immensely helpful in developing your personality. Character-building, right? Quite recently, I had the resolution that some can only dream of when they're dumped. After winning *Drag Race*, I spotted him at Glasgow Central train station.

In my head, this moment of reconciliation would have occurred while I looked my best. However, quite ironically I was wearing a track suit and sweating my absolute tits off. I had no eyebrows and I was tripping over my suitcase. He reached out and congratulated me on my success on the show. It gave me so much closure and helped me to make peace with the unresolved feelings I had from when I was younger. The way you behave in relationships when you're young is daft and should hopefully have no reflection on yourself as an adult.

I cannae be arsed holding a grudge. I used to be a very resentful, hurt person and I projected that onto others. Then I realized, there is no point in me being angry at these people.

Someone messaged me from secondary school and said, 'You are doing such an amazing job, this is the first time I ever watched *Drag Race* and I know this would mean nothing to you, but I just wanted to say I finally get it.' I could easily have said, 'Fuck you, you made my life hell.' But I choose to see the positive. This person now understands something that was so alien to them before that they used it as an excuse to hate. Now, with a new perspective, it will help their kids and people around them to be comfortable in their identity.

If you give someone attention, you have to do it with love. If you want to educate them, they won't respond to you calling them every name under the sun, however tempting it is. Tearing them down won't get you anywhere. This attitude has served me well since being on the show. If my journey can change one person's view of what I do and who I am, then I'm doing something right.

Boyfriend 2: Electric Boogaloo

In the summer of 2016, when I was nineteen years old, I began to date my next boyfriend/victim. This was a two-week relationship – I'm sure you can tell how special it was. Does it even really count? I'm counting it as I've got to get the numbers up. I hadn't been with anyone for ages at this point and was a little jaded over my past experiences. This guy was a really lovely guy and a talented make-up artist who was in the drag scene as well.

The reason I ended up with a significant other on the same drag scene as me is because it's very rare that you will find someone who understands a drag queen's schedule. Try finding a boyfriend who doesn't mind the fact that you are working five nights a week until 3 a.m. We went to the Pride Parade together in Edinburgh, which was also my first ever experience of a Pride event.

I got ready at my friend Alice's house. We watched *Game of Thrones* and were having the time of our lives. I did the march with Alice, then went off and partied with my new man and his friends. After a few drinks, we went back to the hotel to relax and unwind. After a short while of just hanging out, he did the old faithful 'Look what you've done', gesturing to his crotch.

Listen, if I am oversharing, I apologize, but it's my book and I want to be open with you. For that reason I'm going to share with you the cringiest thing I've ever done in my life. Get ready.

I went to town on him, for want of a better word. I was practically playing his penis like a bagpipe when I thought it would be arousing to say the phrase 'I'm gagging on your eleganza.' He froze. I froze. It was the least sexy moment ever. To this day I don't know why I said it. After crying on national television, being bullied in school and being dumped on my birthday, this is still my lowest moment.

A week later, he said we needed space. I don't *think* it was because of the eleganza comment, but I doubt it helped. When he said we needed space, I knew what that meant and just said 'See you later'. I wasn't as hung up this time. Once you've been through heartbreak, it's much easier to recover. I dated a few people after this, but ultimately it's awkward that my drag-career persona has become the third wheel on the date.

The (Dis)honourable Mentions

A few Grindr hits (but mainly misses) later, I met a guy online and we decided to go for a few drinks. I tried to dress up a bit for it, naturally. I pride myself

Right: Two-year-old me in the garden of my gran's house. I could never be stopped from frolicking around and causing mayhem! I would run around the garden shouting 'Exterminate!' at plant pots, and no doubt I was an irritating wee arsehole. Nevertheless, I'm so thankful to have such a supportive, loving family (even though they dressed me like that).

Left: Here we see my wee purple blob of a gran — wearing a cerise cardigan, for once — helping me to improve my drawing skills. This picture sums up our relationship perfectly. She would always help me improve, showing me new techniques and tricks to better my art. If only she knew all the help she'd given me would lead to my drag make-up years later. Cheers for helping me get my eyebrows even, Granny!

Right: My portrait from Stepping Stones Nursery in Helensburgh, 2001. Looking back at this photo makes me a little emotional — when you're that age, you're usually totally unaware of the cruelties of the world and the bullies that you may come to face in the future, so the smile is innocent and genuine. Oh, to be four again. Woft.

Left: Angelina Jolie had nothing on me back in 2003 — I was the OG Maleficent! Thanks to my auntie Dodo for spray-painting and hot-gluing the staff for my Halloween costume. I say this was for Halloween, but I wore this outfit for at least three weeks afterwards, so putting an exact date on this picture is rather difficult.

Right: Just your average after-school activity! Wearing my sister's school dress and my mum's high heels. I think it was evident, even at the age of seven, that I was destined to take over the world and climb my way to stardom, one heeled hoof after the other.

Left: Me, my sister Tamsin, Dad and the wee purple blob on holiday in 2000. Big Phyllis is behind the camera. A cute family picture from afar, but look at me — no doubt I was trying to strangle my dad because I wasn't allowed a Mr Whippy ice cream!

Right: I didn't have designers back in the Halloween of 2004 — my mum made the silver lamé jumpsuit, my dad spray-painted the welly boots and my sister helped me cut a Pringles tube for the gun. I made the chest piece and helmet out of cardboard. Most Cybermen threaten to take over the universe — however, I set my sights on taking over the cookie jar in my gran's house.

Left: I made this ode to the Red Death (*Phantom of the Opera*) and Hamlet's ghost costume out of a red bed sheet. Back in my early days, if the costume could be flailed about, it passed the Lawza test.

Right: My 2010 school portrait from Park House School. Contrary to what it looks like, I did actually brush my hair before the photo was taken. There must have just been static in the air . . .

Left: Little Lawza, aged thirteen. This was an attempt at Lon Chaney from the movie *London After Midnight*. I glued wiry straw to a Smiffys top hat. Looking at this grey straw hair, I realize that not much has changed – just look at my *Drag Race* confessionals . . .

Left: Lawrence Chaney as Jinkx Monsoon as Drew Barrymore as Little Edie from *Grey Gardens*. My first time out in drag — not a wig in sight, just lip gloss, my mum's scarf and a dream.

Right: Alice Rabbit, a knock-off Alaska (aka me) and Axel at AXM in April 2015. The phone that we were trying to take a selfie on fell into one of the Venoms below, so I'm happy we found this snap on Facebook the next day.

Left: August 2018, walking offstage after performing at the Glasgow Festival of Drag. Clock to the right, just behind me: a can of Irn-Bru never goes amiss.

Left: The BBC Scotland channel launch, on 24 February 2019. How could I forget? It's only on the backdrop right behind me! I remember making this dress out of four metres of £1.99 fabric, mere hours before the event. She never stopped, kids!

Right: My flatmate Kiko and I, pictured sober at the end of the night – quite a rare occasion.

Left: Plot twist: Elizabeth I and Mary, Queen of Scots did meet . . . in my living room. My drag daughter Paris and I getting ready for the Glasgow show 'Suck' in May 2019.

Left: Mother's Day 2019. Is there a better gift to give your mother than being in full high-whore drag in her front room?!

Right: In Westminster mid-December 2019, where I was on location talking with Rajdeep Sandhu for BBC The Social. There was me thinking I was going for a job interview to be Leader of the Opposition . . .

Above: Pictured, you can see some of the crew and all cast members (with the exception of Ginny who was having a shite during this). This was just after we wrapped the official BBC Three promotional video for *Drag Race UK* Season 2. If you're wondering why I don't have a wig on . . . You try falling seventeen times off a bucking bronco decorated as bagpipes! Not pictured, the goats, puppies and horse that also cameoed in the video.

Right: Lorraine – with the wean. My showbiz mum, Lorraine Kelly, and I at the 2021 Student Pride event in Heaven, London. This was actually an outtake from our yearbook photoshoot . . . but don't tell anyone!

Left: Little black dress? More like big black dress! Here's a snap of me walking the BAFTA's 2021 Red Carpet. You'll be pleased to hear that the carpet was, in fact, shaved. This look was a tribute to Thalia, the muse of comedy from Greek mythology – and I fancy myself a wee bit of a comedy muse.

Right: In Manchester at the Kimpton Clocktower Hotel, on 18 March 2021, the day I actually found out that I won *Drag Race UK*. Surprise, shock and a bit of pee. Good thing that my pads soaked it up! Multipurpose.

An excited Bimini, an ecstatic Tayce, a tearful Lawza and a seemingly furious Ellie Diamond. I think we were all just happy and emotional because we knew that the 7 a.m. wake-up calls were over.

Mel Gibson as William Wallace in *Braveheart*. Oh wait . . . it's me, Lawrence Chaney, the UK's next *Drag Race* superstar, fae Helensburgh! What a full-circle moment to not only be wearing my gran's signature colour of purple (Mary, please don't sue me) but also to be crowned winner of my favourite TV show! Dreams do come true. Keep blending your eyeshadow, kids!

on being a great judge of character, so I can normally tell if it'll be a winner only a few minutes into the date.

On this occasion, the guy in question was kind of quiet. When I'm faced with an awkward silence, I do what I do best: I start talking shite. Half an hour passed and my back was killing me from the weight of carrying this full conversation. Eventually, after what seemed like an eternity, he asked me what I did for a living.

Now this is where things normally go one of two ways. A potential love interest will either be put off by drag or they will absolutely love it. So I'm waiting for him to tell me he's an absolute *Drag Race* superfan or that he's 'not really into all that'.

Instead, he pulls out his phone and Googles me. I'm just sitting there hoping I've not got any leaked nudes or mug shots floating around the web. It's a bizarre experience for someone to Google you when they are actually sat in front of you having a conversation. Whatever you need to know you can just ask, I am sat right here!

At this point in my career, I was well known on the Glasgow drag scene and I'd done some odd bits and bobs for BBC the Social. I'd say I was probably on the less-than-Z-list at this point, which is much different from the D-List on which I now reside. So as far as I was concerned, I wasn't a big deal.

However, this guy seemed pretty impressed. He suddenly couldn't shut up. Barely a peep out of him for the best part of the hour, but now he was suddenly acting like we're on *Piers Morgan's Life Stories*. 'Have you met any RuPaul queens?' 'How much do you earn?' 'What's your national insurance number and date of birth?'

Well, I made up the last bit, but you get the gist. This was the first time I noticed another human being having an interest in me because of any kind of status. I wasn't even 'famous' back then, but even the mere mention of any kind of notoriety, amongst even the smallest of communities, had someone looking at me differently. That was an immediate red flag. What if I'm an arsehole and we have nothing in common?

Do they love Lawrence Chaney the performer, the character, or do they love what they consider the 'real me'? It's a tricky one because my identity in drag is woven into my identity out of it. Each part of me makes up the whole Lawrence.

When the element of status that comes with successful drag is thrown into the mix, I am doubtful of people who approach me in a romantic sense. Despite our striking resemblance, I'm no' a Kardashian. You're not going to get a trip to the Maldives with me. My budget is more tailored towards a jaunt to Blackpool. But I do wonder if people want something from me that isn't just my friendship.

I also have my reservations when it comes to trusting people further into the relationship, something I'm always working on. Another previous boyfriend had a really detrimental effect on my mental health. It put me off dating for a while and really warped my sense of what a relationship is meant to feel like. Being constantly put down about your appearance when you already don't love what you see in the mirror left me at a bit of a loose end.

With most unhealthy relationships, you don't want to leave them because when it's good it's great. The 'love-bombing' phase really sucks you in. When you are given all this attention for the first time in your life, it feels like a dopamine hit. You try and ignore all the warning signs because it feels better to have the good side of a relationship some of the time than not having it at all.

Well, surprise, this is what a toxic relationship looks like. I hate using the word 'toxic' because it's so overused nowadays. People will say 'My mum's just asked me to take the bins out, she's so toxic', but I think it's the only appropriate word to describe that relationship I was in. I can dust myself off and get back in the saddle now, but it takes time to rebuild trust in yourself and others.

Swipe Right for Your Next Soulmate

Whenever I've found myself single and ready for a Pringle, I've gone looking for love the modern way – oan the apps. Whether it's Grindr, Tinder, Bumble,

Plenty of Fish or Deliveroo, it all boils down to the same conclusion – too much hassle. I think these apps are great for people that are the shy and introverted type, or people who are less likely to meet someone organically in their everyday life. For me, it's all a bit awkward and forced. It gets really depressing when you find yourself resetting the app or joining a new one and you're telling yourself, *Maybe somebody who swiped left me the first time will fancy me now I've got a new profile picture.*

It can also feel very vacuous and repetitive. Once you've read five profiles on Tinder, you've read them all, so here's some tips on how to create a decent dating profile. I cannae promise you'll be successful, but you definitely won't look like a fanny. My biggest pet peeve has got to be when people have the same over-used tagline in their bios. 'Just want to leave the single market before the UK does.' We've heard it before, hen. It wasn't funny the first time and it's certainly not now.

This one is maybe more for the straight boys, but for the love of fuck please don't upload a picture of you handling a fish in any capacity. Nobody wants to see that. Same goes for any of you that have a group of ten friends in your profile pictures. If I wanted that, I'd be on a different app. (Scribbling your friends out of said picture doesn't count either.)

Speaking of Grindr, it has served its purpose for me on a few occasions, but unfortunately I just don't think BigDick29 is going to be my soulmate. We've come a long way in terms of technological advances in society, but I think dating apps could be doing with a bit of regression. I'm not a prude by any means, but the small chat you get on Grindr is pure mental. Someone will pop up and their first message will be, 'Show hole.'

Come on now, at least take me for a drink first.

Then you've got the 'discreet' lads. I've spent too much time embracing and loving my queerness to deal with someone who wants me to be discreet. In my twenty-four years on this earth, not once has the word 'discreet' ever been used to describe me. I wish you well and hope you can find the courage to live your truth one day. It ain't easy, so if you're looking for a helping hand and a guide, I'm your gal, but I'm not looking for a man who wants to push me back into the closet.

Nowadays, people are more likely to pop up and ask me about *Drag Race*, which is fine but also that's no' really why I'm here. Maybe save your questions for my next Instagram Live?

When I decide to stop being a picky bastard and actually match with someone, my complaining starts all over again. There is nothing I hate more than the awkward small chat of the first conversations. The 'What you up to tonight?' just doesn't work for me. Are you going to be my husband or not? Cut to the chase and let me know. I'd rather meet you in person and get to know you there. On a few occasions that is exactly what I've done.

If you've ever built up the confidence to message someone first on a dating app, you will likely have felt the brunt of the humbling experience of getting patched/pied/dingied/ignored/left on read. We've all done it, but as soon as you are on the receiving end you can't help but feel like a bit of a loser. After *Drag Race* aired, I had people who had ignored my messages popping up giving it 'Hey, just seen this sorry, how are you?' Hen, it's been two years . . . What the fuck were you doing, waxing your arsehole? Building up the confidence to message back? Save the excuses, I'd rather you were just upfront and said, 'I don't fancy you, but now you are on the telly I want to shag you.'

I value honesty. If you want to be a starfucker, then just admit it. Of course, I never message these people back because as Marilyn Monroe famously said, 'If you can't handle me at my Barry M, you don't deserve me at my Anastasia Beverly Hills', or whatever the quote is.

It's nice to have a good old cackle at your phone and just think *#Get fucked*. I'm only putting out positive vibes and trying to embody a PMA (positive mental attitude – thanks, Bimini), so I don't actually reply with any ill wishes, I just leave them on read. There is something so sweet about seeing yourself go from the patchee to the patcher. I feel like this is my villain origin story. I was ignored one too many times and then became a famous drag queen just to spite them. If anybody wants to buy the rights to that story, it's yours for the small fee of one million doll hairs.

I have since returned to trying my luck at dating apps and casual hook-ups. One thing I will say about it all is that it's given me some good stand-up material. One guy brought me back to his house and we were about to make sweet drag-queen love when suddenly I heard a door slam in the other room. It came to an abrupt stop when he said, 'This isn't actually my house, it's my sister's, you need to leave.' I thought, *Fucking hell, well, you can pay my Uber.*

Grindr has been difficult to navigate for me since being on the television. Someone messaged me: 'Hey, how are you doing, Mrs Ru Queen winner of Glasgow.' Is that not the most awkward introduction to someone? What on earth do I respond to that?

When it comes to *Drag Race*, people either can't stop talking about it or avoid the subject completely. Sometimes people introduce themselves with a 'Hey, queen!' (which can mean many things in this community . . .). I'm not sure if they are aware or not that I am a drag queen and spend the rest of the convo trying to suss it out.

It's got to the point where I no longer message someone first. It can be a bit awkward. You are always concerned if people are going to screenshot something or send it to their friends, so you don't want to open up about anything too personal. There is also the risk that people are messaging you just to be like 'OMG, I've been chatting to Lawrence Chaney on Grindr, I matched with them on Tinder', as opposed to because they actually find you attractive.

People have seen me at my worst and at my best on national television, so this means a lot of strangers know everything about me. It's such a strange and imbalanced way to start off meeting someone.

Another thing I've experienced is people on the apps acting extra masc, as if they'd never have watched *Drag Race* before. They'll say stuff like 'Hello, my guy. Hello, my bud, buddy, bro.' Then when you invite them over, they just want to see behind the scenes so they can get a look at my wigs or wear my RuPeter badges.

I had someone over once and just moments before coitus they uttered the words, 'I can't believe I'm shagging Lawrence Chaney.' What a turn-off. I immediately said 'Right, get out!' Get out of me and out of my house!

This was before *Drag Race*, so imagine the risk of that happening now!

On top of all that, there is always the fear that someone will share screenshots of your pictures or messages. Before *Drag Race*, I would be lending my toad-in-a-hole-looking kabussy pic out to anyone who would ask. Nowadays, there is no chance. I shudder to think of the nudes that are probably circling. Fear of being leaked aside, the nudes in general can put you off Grindr – if you are looking for a less abrupt and sexualized conversation. You might then switch to Tinder in the hopes of a slightly more personal experience.

The problem I have with Tinder is that it's seen as this upper-class Grindr. You have to verify your email, which means you're not a serial killer. Which I suppose is a pro. But after that, it's just a glorified Grindr. Everyone just wants to get pumped, whether they act like it or not. At least on Grindr people are upfront. I spoke to someone on Tinder before who had no interest in dating me or publicly proclaiming that he found me attractive. I think it's harder to trust because you can't send photos. It's hard to know you are not being cat-fished, so people who might not have come out yet are much more hesitant about opening up. On the other hand, it's promiscuous and direct on Grindr, but you do put yourself in danger. I'd rather give my jewels up to someone trying to rob me rather than fight for my possessions.

Sometimes people have faceless profiles but a gorgeous body. Often this means they have a killer body but the face is yikes, so they leave it out. Or if you're like me, both the body and face are yikes. What can I say? We work with what we have.

I've had people over who looked nothing like their picture. It was like an entirely different person; he had a pubey beard and looked like Jasmine Masters on the Bearded Runway. In cases like these, you find yourself in a position where you feel like you have to sleep with someone because they are here now and it might be too awkward to say you aren't feeling it.

Remember that you can always change your mind, so don't shy away from it. Just because someone paid for a bus ticket doesn't mean you need to go for a ride. Nowadays I just tell people straight if I'm no longer interested. Even if they're already stood naked in my bedroom, it doesn't matter. If you don't feel it, don't do it.

Returning to the Dating Lyfe

Not long before The Call, I did venture once more into the breach. This person did drag as well, and I had geared myself up to get back into dating. It was an awful experience and had me a complete mess mentally. They were telling me they were hooking up with people hours before our dates and then making me out to be a psycho for having a problem with that. I think you'd agree that if someone is showing up to the date having been pumped an hour prior, it's not good vibes. They even brought along someone else they were dating to my own drag show. It was just really horrible. The uncertainty was getting to me, but I so badly wanted something to work I just put up with this shit.

I used to ignore my own feelings of awkwardness,

just so the dynamic and atmosphere was more comfortable for the other person. This also applies to dates: I'd speak and fill in the gaps so the other person felt more relaxed.

The only exception to this is when I'm at the cinema. A story comes to mind, actually. On one of our dates, we went to see a horror film. I'm a big horror fan, so I was concentrating hard on the movie and this guy was just trying to munch on my face. Listen, I've got popcorn, a hotdog, nachos and a Tango Ice Blast (and that's just the appetizer!). I don't need you leaning over my food that cost me a small fortune trying to neck on with me. I want to watch the film, hen.

On one particular Thursday night I was performing at Trigger. I was feeling quite low because my date had arrived with the guy they were shagging. Imagine someone you are seeing shagging someone else and bringing them to your workplace. Earlier that day, they had asked me to meet up before the show and then had the gall to say that I was ignoring them. Trying to insinuate that it was my fault and not theirs was a common occurrence in this relationship. I went home early because I was shattered and feeling defeated. My flatmate came home and told me that she saw them getting together in the club. You can imagine the emotional state I was in. I thought, *Nobody loves me. I am a waste of space.*

I was worried for my mental health because I had

constantly been fucked over by men like this. I didn't have a single successful story in love and romance. How could I live my dream life when nobody was interested in me?

I stayed up all night crying and listening to Celine. I really was trying to marry the night. I woke my flatmate up, crying because nobody loved me. It was a long night for both of us. I woke up the next morning feeling like a zombie, until I got a text at 10:38 saying, 'Hey, it's the Drag Race team, can we call you?'

I jumped up and texted back faster than you can say gasbag. 'Yes, I'm free now.'

My job means that I'm booked and busy and have little free time, so finding a significant other often goes on the back burner. (Yeah, I know, I hate the term 'booked and busy' an' aw. Anyone that says they are booked and busy has two gigs lined up for the rest of the year. Apart from me, of course. Insert villainous cackle here.) I'm a very career-orientated person, so my first priority will always be having a roof over my head and food in my three fridges. Finding someone to slot into that lifestyle ain't easy.

Queens spend most of their life in nightclubs, so it's like permanently being on the nightshift. Clubs also aren't the dream location to meet potential suitors. Especially since I'm either in full drag or my make-up's melting off my mug and my tit plate is hinging oot. (Thanks, Jim Carrey in *The Mask*.) The music is too loud and I can't hear a word anyone is saying. It's just not ideal when someone is introducing themselves and I'm competing with Ariana Grande on the speaker. I end up screaming 'WIT?! I CAN-NAE HEAR YE!'

Don't get me wrong, I'm partial to a wee disco winch (a kiss on the dance floor) and queer nightlife is a great place to do this safely and securely without worrying about getting gay-bashed. However, at the ripe age of twenty-four (which is nearly 100 in gay years), I think those days are behind me. If you've found your partner in lesbian corner, then I salute you. It's a graft I can't be bothered to put in. Maybe I'm just lazy when it comes to love and that's the problem. Either way, it's not something I prioritize or actively seek out any more. World domination comes first.

Dating Dos and Don'ts

✓ **DO** know your worth. Never let anyone tell you that you aren't good enough or aren't worthy of love. It doesn't matter how gorgeous they are or how much you think they're your next soulmate. If they are an arsehole, don't excuse their behaviour. You're incredible and worthy of respect and a bloody good shag.

✓ **DO** let people in. We've all been burned before, but this isn't a reason to cut yourself off from everyone. I know what it feels like to think *Fuck that, I'm not going to put myself at risk of being dumped and heartbroken again.* I promise the high is worth the pain.

✓ **DO** be honest about drag. As much as you might think you could keep it a secret, they are probably going to find out. It's a big part of your identity and potentially your future career. I'm telling you: those fake lashes end up everywhere. Be upfront about why you love it. If they are put off by this, they're probably harbouring some internalized homophobia, so you've dodged a bullet.

✓ **DO** communicate. We've all had a date that has been a complete flop. If you are not feeling it, be kind and respectful and let them down gently. Don't say you want to be pals if you don't want to be. Don't say yes to another date if you were bored out of your mind on the first one. Effective communication will solve most of life's problems and save you from a lot of awkward trips to Nando's.

✓ **DO** leave the drag out of the bedroom. Unless you're both into that, leave your 'Yass, mama, slay!' comments for when you are out with the gals, not for when you are getting your back blown out. May I refer you back to the Eleganza Incident of '16.

✘ **DON'T** wear your pads on a date. Some shallow potential lovers may be disappointed to find out your arse isn't what it appears to be.

✘ **DON'T** hold grudges. The scene is way too small in your local area to have a vendetta against another queer person. Try and keep the post-break-up bitching to a minimum. One of your pals will know them to some extent. If you have an unpleasant date with them, tell your close pals if you fancy it, but don't try to exile them from the whole community. Life is too short to hold a grudge.

✘ **DON'T** date their family. No, not like that. Though don't do that either! What I mean is, don't stay in a relationship with someone purely because you like their maw or their maw likes you.

✘ **DON'T** ask to see their phone. Keep a level head. You should trust them to make the right decision and avoid temptation. Try not to fall into the trap of looking through your significant other's phone. It's not worth it and it's not a good look. If you don't trust them, you've got other issues to deal with.

✗ **DON'T** take someone to the cinema on a
date if you don't want to watch the film. OK,
I know I've already mentioned this, but I'm
still annoyed. Seriously, if I'm going to the
cinema I'm going to eat my snacks and watch
the film. There will be no kissing or touching,
thanks.

7
0-100 in the Drag Race

Here, we talk about *Drag Race* so much, it's a wonder that those outside of our circles don't think we're all Vin Diesel wannabes, street-racing in Japanese import cars and souped-up Corsas. It cannot be denied, *RuPaul's Drag Race* truly has changed the landscape of drag for ever and has opened up the art form to so many more. Taking us from dive bars to live stars, *Drag Race* has helped expand communities of queer people and given so many people spaces to be themselves. To be completely honest with you, *Drag Race UK* is the only thing I've ever successfully topped.

I might have been a fan for years, but the experience itself is something entirely different. I'm going to take you through from when I was preparing for the show, my thoughts and feelings from each episode, the Covid-19 break and winning! It's time for the whistle-stop tour. Get your seatbelt on – it's gonna be a bumpy ride!

My Drag Race Obsession isn't about Cars, Honest

I started watching *Drag Race* while Season 4 was airing. I was shocked — up until this point, I thought drag was only for middle-aged men in paillette-covered dresses, telling jokes in the local to a room full of football fans and their pints. Far from it! The show led me to a world where drag wasn't limited by gender, and there wasn't only one way to be a drag artist. After consuming every episode, untucked, meet the queens, behind the scenes . . . I really Sasha Belle'd it and thought I might have cracked the code. Oh, hen, how wrong I was.

Preparing for the Race

I'll remember the day I received The Call for the rest of my days. All manner of emotions flow through you — excitement, anxiety, disbelief, denial, relief. Up until this point, my two emotions were tired or hungry, and even both on some days, so you can imagine how much of a shock to the system this was. Knowing that one of my childhood idols had watched my audition tape and gave it the green light . . . It was insane.

It's so strange to think about how a phone call can change your life overnight as well. Last night I was crying because nobody loved me, and today I was crying because my lifetime dream and aspiration was coming true.

There's not long to soak it in and let it become real, because from the second The Call ends, the countdown clock begins. Every favour in the book was called in, all under the guise of an 'upcoming project' that I was working on. My friend Conor was on the sewing machine, with my other friend Kim stoning the garment as it came through. My drag daughter, Paris, was on the other sewing machine, while my flatmate, Kiko, reset every wig in my inventory and ran to Primark to buy every set of false nails in the shop. (A quick note to any visiting drag artist from overseas – hit Primark for your nails. Every colour imaginable, printed nails, stoned nails, all for under £2 a pop.) My friend Perry was cutting me new pads while my pal Kelsay drained drag supply shops of their jewels. If you're wondering why there was a rhinestone shortage in haberdasheries in Glasgow in early 2020, I raise my hands. Guilty as charged.

Suddenly my living room had a new feature, based on sketches of potential looks and ideas. It was like a detective's push-pinned crazy wall. Trying to produce so many designs in three seconds flat is not easy on the brain either. How do you encapsulate a day at the seaside into a dress? Stoned on the runway . . . should I get 4/20 blazing? Despite the struggle, I managed to pull my designs together by taking inspiration from some of my favourite pop-culture references and paying tribute to my previous looks, performances and, of course, my country. References from *The Avengers*, *Doctor Who* and Charles Rennie Mackintosh can be seen throughout my runways – Mrs Peel's iconic catsuit and bowler hat, Eldrad – now in pink! – from the original *Who* broadcasts, transforming a Mackintosh stained-glass window into a latex gown. I didn't just try to meet the definitions of the categories, I wanted to fully encapsulate how Lawrence Chaney would look in every theme.

After all my wigs were cleaned and straightened out, they had to be styled. Yet another mammoth task. Ordering styled wigs is an option but considering that everybody is going away at the same time, if you're not fast, you're wigless. At that point it was one year BDR (Before *Drag Race*). Ellie Diamond was the gal to go to if you needed wigs turned out from flat to fabulous in about forty seconds flat. I called her up.

'Hey, babes, I've got a big project coming up and I need a few wigs for it. Would you be able to help?'

'Ehhh, well, babes, I also have a big project coming up and I'm already going to be styling a lot of wigs.'

I froze. Ellie wasn't talking about taking a year out to style wigs for an off-West End version of *Cinderella*. She, too, was going away. With a sigh, I picked up the teasing brush.

Tits? In My Hand Luggage?

Hours before I was due to depart, I was still packing. I know you might not know if you want to take the pink or blue bikini with you to Magaluf and end up spending two days fixating on it, but take my word for it – this is a new breed of evil. We all joke about going over baggage allowance at the airport, opening your suitcase and putting on all of your clothes to avoid paying the extra weight allowance – but when I say that was a genuine consideration, I'm not kidding. I crammed the vast majority of my runways into a couple of suitcases, packing just enough underwear to get me through filming, and created a plastic storage contraption out of two boxes and cable ties for my wigs.

Fuck knows how they got that on the poor Boeing 747. I wish I had thrown different outfits out the window as I flew over the United Kingdom. I would've had much less to work with on the show, but chucking my arse padding over the M6 would've been a right laugh. Maybe next time.

I almost quit the whole thing when I was going through security. I had run out of space in my main luggage and had to resort to stuffing various items into my carry-on. One of these items happened to be a silicone breastplate. Oh, of course it went exactly how you imagined it. Not only did they almost fall out of the bag on my way to security, but when I placed the bag on the scanner belt, I felt only dread. I knew it was coming. I walked through the body scanner and saw my bag being pulled to the side for inspection. I was called over, and out came the tits, nipples and all. How could I think that was going to go well? Tits? In my hand luggage? I managed to blab my way out of it and luckily didn't go down for being a drug mule. I can just see the headlines now. 'Disgraced Scottish drag queen caught with 24 pounds' worth of breast in airport crackdown.' My smuggling career is on hold for the moment. I'm too anxious to try it again. I still get the total fear thinking about this. What if my debut on national television was *UK Border Force* instead of *Drag Race*?!

My Packing Dos and Don'ts

✓ **DO** get used to Tetris-style packing. This works totally against my usual style of furiously balling-up my outfits and shoving them into cases – it's just not intuitive. When your arse (padding) is the size of Ben Nevis, you need to pack intelligently.

✓ **DO** bring porn. It's the 2020s. Hotel rooms don't have porn available on the channels any more, and that's no wanking for you if you forget. The last thing you need when you're away for so long is blue balls (unless that's a runway theme). An essential use of your limited packing time is burning *Dirty Doctors 4* onto a disc for your portable DVD player.

✓ **DO** pack an MP3 player, preferably with *Chromatica* on it. I know, you've not used an MP3 player since you were sixteen, pirating Britney's new singles on Limewire – but what's a gal to do? You're going to need something to help you de-stress, or amp you up. Personally, I find nothing more invigorating than the transition from 'Chromatica II' to '911'.

✗ **DON'T** forget your nails. It's like when you arrive in the south of France and cannae charge your phone because you forgot to bring a UK–Europe power converter. Except, instead of your phone dying, you get to walk down the runway with your un-manicured, stubby wee nails. Poor Kiko, I made her buy Glasgow's entire stock of press-ons, for nothing!

✗ **DON'T** bring Christian Louboutin's entire back catalogue of heels. Shoes take up more space than you'd imagine, so think smart. Bring heels that match a variety of looks – I went for nude, black, white and Perspex. I had some runway-specific heels, but when I needed a good pump for a mini challenge (mind out of the gutter), I would be able to rely on these.

I'm Like the Loch Ness Monster . . . A Legend

Everything started to get a little more real when I was arriving at the hotel room. By 'real', I mean that I was snapped out of my daze by near-enough respiratory arrest trying to get my suitcases up the bloody stairs. I arrived and flopped onto my bed. Even though the actual challenges hadn't started yet, weeks of preparing had already taken a bit of a toll on me. There was no 'settling in', and that wee moment when you explore the facilities of your room – exhaustion took over and that didn't happen.

The next day was an early one. It was entrance day, and call time was early. Naturally, filming a show isn't like your usual wee 9 to 5 doon the Littlewoods – unless by 9 to 5 you mean 9 o'clock in the morning until 5 o'clock the next morning. I had to be up at the arsecrack of dawn to start getting ready. Now, I'm saddened to inform you, I do suffer from a chronic illness. It's affectionately named 'Fuck-I'm-Going-To-Sleep-In-Tomorrow-I-Need-To-Get-Up-At-2-a.m.-itis'. It's quite rare, I don't expect you to have heard of it. After three cans of Red Bull, however, you couldn't tell I was essentially unconscious anyway. You might have seen a faint outline of my heart beating in my chest, but what's drag without a caffeine overload?

My entrance look was something I had been

considering for months before I even knew I had been cast. I wanted it to be unexpected, new. Back in Scotland, I had been performing up to five nights a week for a while, and I think people might have got quite used to seeing me in sequin muumuus and simpler gowns – hen, gran had to be comfortable, or she'd throw her bad hip out. Again. The time for comfort was over.

Bright purple. Boot covers. Perfectly flush to the body, except for a sewn-in skirt that cut just above the thigh. Head to toe, obnoxious print. Gold detail. Flame sunglasses. I had never worn anything like it, yet it was still undeniably a Lawrence Chaney look. If there's anything I love, it's seeing the garment go from design to pattern pieces cut out on the floor, to fully fitted and constructed. It's why I recommend learning how to sew so much! It's such a rewarding process.

Now, while I had been considering my entrance look for a few months, I knew what I wanted my entrance line to be for two years. I shudder to think, what if someone got on before me and made a Loch Ness joke? There's no' exactly much to pull from in Scotland that people have a chance of understanding all around the globe. Haggis. Whisky. Kilts. Robert the Bruce. Those aren't exactly thrilling choices either. What would I end up saying?

'I was going to bring haggis, but I don't have the *stomach* for it!' See? Weak.

I had been practising the line in question about a thousand times a day, walking from the kitchen to the front room and back again. I can only apologize to Kiko for this. Anyway, there I was, sitting in the holding area, awaiting my fate. In the distance, I heard the slightly muffled noise of what must have been a test run.

'Her Majesty's done already done had herses!'

The reality of the situation hit me like a crate of RuPaul Iron Fist heels. I was about to take the first steps on the moon, go where no Scottish queen had ever gone before. *Drag Race*: the Final Frontier.

I was escorted from the room to a dimly lit corridor. Some might be spooked by this, but I've been watching horror films since I came out the womb. Nothing could scare me now. I only had one shot at this and I had to make it count. I got the nod, worked up every ounce of confidence I had, and stomped into the bright pink Werk Room of *RuPaul's Drag Race UK*.

'I'm like the Loch Ness Monster . . . A legend!'

Ready, Set . . .

Sitting watching the other queens enter the room was a surreal and lucky experience – I got to size up everyone, one by one, seeing who was going to fall first and who I was going to drop pearls under. I'm just kidding, it wasn't like that at all! The first day is great, because everyone is at their best and ready for the competition. I saw some performers I knew, and some I was meeting for the first time, so I was kept guessing.

Cherry Valentine was the first to walk into the room, and didn't she come with a bang? Literally. Somebody from the production team should have really sent her the measurements of the doorway. Cherry is pure eye candy to me. Every look is drop-dead gorgeous, thought out from head to toe, and executed perfectly. After meeting her, I set out on a journey to answer one of life's big questions. Do they have good teeth in Darlington?

Tia Kofi was next. Despite what you might have seen on the show, Tia is one of my closest friends now – and it's not just because we share a government name! Tia is someone who never fails to make me laugh with a quick and sharp wit, and my God, she's got a set of lungs on her! Seconds after Tia reads East London drag artists, in walks the plant-based princess . . .

Bimini Bon Boulash. Adorned in a nude illusion, pink leather scenario, I think Bimini might have one of the best entrance lines in the history of *Drag Race*. In that moment, I had no idea Bimini was such a multi-faceted drag artist. They're a true triple threat – a model, a rapper and one of the bendiest bitches I know. Bimini is kindness personified; I honestly don't think they have a bad bone in their body. They really are one of my pals, and when we did go for nuggets I made sure they were Quorn.

A blur of yellow, and I knew immediately who was about to step into the Werk Room and what was about to come out of their mouth. It's only Ginny Lemon! Ginny was one of the first performers I watched when I began venturing outside of Scotland, and when you hear the screech of 'Fancy a slice?!' you'll never be able to get it out of your head. I am also a personal fan of their hit single, 'Woolworths'. Be warned: once you listen to it, there's no going back.

Now, when you see something that is eight feet tall, pink and gingham, you know exactly who it is. The Baby Doll of Dundee, Ellie Diamond. Keeping a straight face and pretending I hadn't figured out Ellie was also at 'summer camp' was not easy. Ellie is someone who practically came out of nowhere in Scotland. One day she was a budding baby queen, but overnight she seemed to take to sewing and wig styling and became a fully blossomed adult baby queen!

A bag with a blue circle motif with lips inside, it was Sister Sister that walked into the Werk Room. I had no idea that later in that episode she would give me such an important and meaningful piece of advice and encouragement. Despite being someone that feels at home in front of a camera, taking the face off the first time was nerve-wracking, and Sister helped me through that. Also, can we talk about how she's the first ever to lip-sync alone?!

I think her hair hit my face before she even made it into the room. With long, luscious hair like that and those legs, of course it was Tayce. The lip-sync assassin herself! I had previously met Tayce at Drag World in 2018. She didn't remember meeting me. I don't know if that meant I was forgettable, or she was so off her tits on Red Bull that she blacked out. Where do you think her tagline, the Energizer Bunny of Drag, comes from?

A true cabaret legend followed. The one and only Joe Black. Joe had been performing up and down the country from before I was born, so seeing her saunter into the room was surreal. I'm so glad we were on together, because the show brought us closer together in a big way. I don't know why I'm complimenting her, though. The first thing she did upon seeing me was look me up and down and say, 'God, this print is hideous.'

'It's time to get this party started. Right now!'

I'll excuse the fact that Veronica Green (affectionately dubbed 'Ronnie') stole my colour when she entered the arena. Little did I know, I would be quoting that line for months, and one of my top priorities when going to shows after *Drag Race* was seeing Ronnie belt out 'Get The Party Started'. She's got the range.

I had been watching the subsequent entrant, Asttina Mandella, for a couple of years before the show. She was one of the first people that brought true voguing up to Scotland when she visited – not the flapping you see some people do. With legendary skills like hers, I immediately retired any choreography I had learned before coming on the show, on the spot. No questions asked.

Finally, into the Werk Room, clicking her heels three times, it was A'Whora. A'Whora didn't just bring looks, she brought *looks*. Everything she wears is finished to absolute perfection, and I think I'm going to have to poach her wig designer because her hair is honestly spectacular.

We all had a moment to gather round the table and have a quick gab before the starting siren played. We all ran over, lining up in front of the steps. We knew exactly what came next.

Her Royal Highness, RuPaul

They say don't meet your idols. I'm telling you now, that is absolute pish. Meeting RuPaul still seems surreal to me. Seeing someone so successful, at the top of their game, but who still retains such kindness and professionalism, is so inspiring. I'm saying all this as if it was our first meeting, though, when we've actually been well acquainted since 2015. That was the year *Drag Race* officially began airing on a UK TV network. RuPaul and other amazing drag artists were plastered over buses, billboards and backdrops all across the country. Well, eighteen-year-old Lawza couldn't cope. I had to have her.

My aunt happened to work for a bus company at the time. You see where this is going, don't you? That's right, I acquired a life-size RuPaul cut-out, from the side of your local Arriva bus, which, to this day, lives in my bedroom. Yep. In my shoebox shitehole wee flat in Glasgow, I still have RuPaul nailed to my bedroom wall. Unless you know somebody else that had the same idea, I think it's pretty likely that this might be one of the most exclusive pieces of RuPaul merch out there.

I did have a little bit of concern that Ru might not understand my dulcet Glaswegian tones. However, from the very first 'LAWWHRENCE CHANEEEH!' that thought was dashed.

Little did I know, that would be the first of many. That reminds me of a funny story, actually. Throughout my years performing up and down the UK, for some reason, people seem to have really struggled with my name. I've been introduced as Lawrence Channy, Lance Chansey, Chorence Laney . . . The list goes on. I've never understood this. I didn't think my name was particularly hard to say! I have to say, I'm immensely thankful to RuPaul for putting this debate to bed, once and for all.

You might think RuPaul would be exhausted – she's constantly flying around the world and filming so many different things. If she is, she damn sure doesn't show it! I really have to take a leaf out of her book on this one – you can see from a mile away that I'm a dour-faced bastard when I'm tired. I felt a real connection to Ru and the other judges on the show. I really felt like they understood me as a drag artist and what I wanted to achieve with my career. As I've said already, one of my absolute greatest joys in life is making other people laugh – the fact that I had them going at every corner means so much to me. Especially as someone who brands themselves as a comedian, it's the most sweet, sweet validation I could have ever wished for.

. . . *Go!*

The challenges started, thick and fast, and, before we knew it, we were already on to the first elimination. Episode one's challenges were a photoshoot and a runway, and I felt at ease immediately. Thank God they weren't shoving a microphone in front of my mouth and expecting me to sing like a canary from day one. (Little did I know what day two would bring . . .) After some jumbo tennis balls nearly dislodged my jaw and popped a hernia, we walked the runway in the 'UK Gay Icon' and 'Queen of Your Hometown' categories.

I didn't want to be predictable in either category and go for a traditional gay icon, or walk the runway in tartan. Instead, I chose to walk first in a skin-hugging catsuit in tribute to the late Diana Rigg. From when I was young and watched *The Avengers*, I was obsessed with every look she wore on that show, and I knew the look would be both unique and unexpected from me.

Next, I slid into a floor-sweeping latex creation, designed after one of Glasgow's most legendary architects and designers, Charles Rennie Mackintosh. When I was young, my mum used to work in the Hill House in Helensburgh. This is one of Mackintosh's greatest masterpieces and introduced me to the intricacies and wonders of his design skill.

I was very proud with what I presented on the runway and getting through the first week safely was the best I could have hoped for. Something that I wasn't quite prepared for was stepping to the back of the stage and watching my first ever 'Lip Sync for Your Life' in person. It was Bimini vs Joe, and I had no idea how to feel. Both put up a brilliant fight, but that didn't change how absolutely heart-wrenching it was to see Joe walk away first.

There wasn't time to grieve for our losses before episode two came around and brought my two weaknesses together – singing and dancing. The tears I cried during rehearsal were very real. I didn't yet know how to break through the barrier that told me I couldn't sing or dance – all I knew was that I was awful at it. Instead of thinking of ways I could camp it up and change the brief to my needs, I let myself get defeated by 'Rats: the Rusical'.

I do feel as though my runway may have saved my skin. It was the 'Surprise, Surprise' category: our best two-in-one look. While others may have opted for tear-away style reveals, I knew I wanted a fully purpose-made two-in-one costume. On the first layer, bright blue sequins and a white bias binding, representing the Scottish flag. Were the trousers tearaways? Nope, it was the sleeves! With a spin, I was gliding down the runway in bold tartan, fixing my bow in my hair.

Walking the main stage in *Drag Race* is surreal. When you step out onto the stage, you're blinded by the harsh, burning lights. With one step forward, you need to quickly find your rhythm with the music – often I'd find myself trying to hit every beat with a stomp of my heels, or at least every second! You pose and stare the judges down as if your eyes could shoot daggers. Somehow, you have to convince them with a few twirls and a piercing gaze that you are someone worth betting on. Sometimes, you can't help but heckle back a response at some of their critiques.

'I'll show you my shagpipes!'

After narrowly avoiding the bottom two in the previous episode, hearing that a sewing challenge was next up was music to my ears. Something I could sink my teeth into! Ellie and I got the gold box and I immediately cycled through my back catalogue of silhouettes. Having a Rolodex of what works for you with sewing comes over time, after you've tried and failed many a costume. I cannot stress enough how valuable a skill sewing is to have. While you might start on a leotard or bodycon dress, you can move to learning techniques such as lining, ruffling, drop neck-lines and boned corsets. Having an eye for colour is also something insanely important – while everything in the box was gold, there were different tones that may not have paired well with each other. Sewing is one of the only ways to effectively 'study' for *RuPaul's Drag Race*, and if you wanna pass that exam with dis-tinction, then it is truly vital.

This challenge ended up being my first win.

'Fuck me sideways!'

This win marked a turning point in my mindset, when I went from uncertain and nervous to feeling like a real contender. Everyone has a weakness and having mine exploited the week before had really given me a good shake-up, but instead of giving up I let the fall light a fire inside me and came back fighting.

'Morning Glory'! I really hope this challenge was a looking glass into my future because TV hosting is where I would like to be in a few years. Not only that, but being judged by the one and only Lorraine Kelly of all people! She really is the queen of British day-time television. This challenge felt like it came naturally to me – before *Drag Race*, I had the opportunity to do some television work for BBC Scotland. One of these shows was called the *Insider's Guide*, where I took view-ers around some of my favourite spots in Glasgow. I was able to put my presenting skills to the test, and I think it's safe to say I crushed it. No, really. Someone ask *Drag Race* to send me an invoice for that poor tricycle.

I was so ecstatic to bring my 'Monster Mash-up' runway to the stage. Preparing for this was a dream come true. If you've been paying attention so far, you'll know I am a huge horror-film buff. I knew this runway had to be special – Jason Voorhees was practically grunting at me from his special place in hell. In my past, I had countless previous looks and ideas to pull from. I had performed as Pennywise the Dancing Clown on multiple occasions, with a custom-sewn replica of his costume with built-in skirt reveal that had balloons inside. I did an entire make-up series devoted to the re-creation of horror-film characters and posters. Perhaps I had a little too much to pull from.

I brought on my long-time friend and fellow drag artist Axel, to bring this creation to life. I had drawn up a tight-fitting gown made of human flesh. I wanted the edges to be ragged, the skin textured and the seams to be uneven. Leatherface meets haute couture. Axel took a cast of my face, hand and ear (I let him use his own nipple) and used latex to effectively create a full dress out of prosthetics. It was hand-painted, with veins, blemishes and all. I initially thought about wearing a lab coat, but instead I went with a pristine white bodysuit, then splattered it with blood before my friend Kim adorned it with deep red rhinestones. Has blood ever looked so stunning?

I was shocked to walk away with another RuPeter badge. However, watching the elimination was even more gobsmacking. I had very strong feelings about Ginny walking away at the time, but that was my pressured, stressed brain speaking. I understand now why they decided to go – Ginny Lemon lives life on their own terms! They knew they didn't want to go up against one of their closest friends in the competition. While it's not something I would have been able to do myself, I have grown to hugely respect them for this decision.

It was twist after twist that day. Walking back into the Werk Room after Sister's performance, we all sat down and began to hash it out about who should or shouldn't have been in the bottom. Tia and I were just about to go nail-to-nail when the sirens sounded, and everything stopped. The eight of us walked over to the screen.

The Pit Stop - feat. Covid-19

Being told we had to cease filming and return home absolutely popped any high I was experiencing after winning twice in a row. We packed up and returned back home to our lives, and let me tell you, it was strange. Getting back to Glasgow, to my tiny city flat . . . It felt like unfinished business. I wasn't meant to be home yet.

The landscape for the first while was immensely grim. I was a full-time entertainer, with nothing to fall back on. I had used my savings for wigs and fabric. Kiko had just started a new job and had to stop almost immediately, with very little furlough. We both had next to no income and had no idea how to pay the bills. How were we going to put food on the table?

Signing on for financial support was a strange experience for me. I feel like there's this unhealthy stigma around those that need to sign on, and people forget why it actually exists. As with most stereotypes, however, they're a total generalization and very untrue. I'm thankful that we were able to receive the support we needed to keep going and keep a roof over our heads. You've gotta do what you gotta do to survive!

Many people were of the opinion that the break was a perfect time to regroup and rethink your whole plan. I understand why it may seem like the ideal time; however, given the circumstances, I could not disagree more. Think of it like this: why were we on a break? Oh, that's right! The world was essentially ending. The Black Plague Volume 2, the sequel, the remix. Of course, it wasn't actually the apocalypse. However, for performers, it may as well have been.

Quarantine and isolation meant finding the motivation or drive to work on yourself or your skills was very hard. Many days, getting out of bed was the achievement of the day – and I think that's OK. Putting undue pressure on yourself during such a trying and hopeless time feels redundant. After the first few proposed end-of-lockdown dates kept getting pushed back, getting your hopes up for anything only left you with a greater disappointment. I did see many people pick up hobbies they might have not yet had the opportunity to try out – like sewing, or wig styling – but I still strongly think nobody should be putting themselves down for feeling too low to pick up a needle and thread.

What does drag look like when venues close and you can't gather? Not much. On saying this, however, I am endlessly impressed by the resilience of performers around the world. So many of us have such a deep love of drag that just stopping isn't an option. Drag took to the virtual world in a way we had never seen it before. Online shows could have performers from every corner of the globe, performing music video-style. I even tried my hand at transforming my trusty 'Charity Shoap' mix into a video performance, as well as mashing up Madonna's 'Vogue' with the best thing to happen to 2020 – 'Babylon' from *Chromatica*.

The production wasn't quite on a TV studio's level. Kiko and I pinned green fabric from ceiling to floor in our tiny living room and set up some lights. We filmed take after take, look after look, until we felt like we had built up enough footage to squeeze a video out of. From that point on, I admit I was a bit redundant and hoped for the best – when it comes to technology, I'm a bit like your gran. Imagine giving your gran an iPhone and expecting her to seamlessly make a phone call without significant help, as well as trying to explain why there are no buttons. That's me with any sort of technology or DIY task. Hey, you cannae be good at everything!

I left the video in the capable hands of Kiko, who had incidentally learned a fair bit about video editing for her own online performances. A few days later, the videos of me waddling about in front of a scrap of green fabric transformed into something that looked like it was lifted straight out of that 90s music-video set for 'Vogue'. I absolutely loved it, but let me tell you, after all that work, I won't be doing another digital performance any time soon!

I think that's how the entire community started to feel after the first few months of the pandemic. Initially, digital drag was shiny and new, and a great way to continue our art when we couldn't leave our homes. However, as with anything new, the sheen wore off over time. The amount of work to try and simulate the adrenaline of being on the stage wasn't worth it any more – and didn't even come close to how it feels to stand in front of an audience.

As the pandemic continued, the distance from family started to take its toll. I hadn't seen my mum or dad in person since they had delivered some of my mum's wig creations, back before the pandemic. We tried video calls and phone calls, but after a while we ran out of things to talk about. When everything screeches to a halt and life is stuck in suspended animation, thinking up conversation topics was a struggle. There were no new films or TV shows out, no shows to talk about – the only thing left to talk about was when we thought it would be over. That overwhelming feeling of loneliness that has no visible solution is absolutely hellish to experience. The silver lining of that, however, is that everyone was very much in the same boat.

Summer was a nice touch of respite for everyone here in Scotland. We were able to venture outside to parks and gardens, and finally see people we hadn't seen in what felt like a lifetime. I'm personally not inclined to the sunlight, but I braved the UV rays for a much-needed chance to connect with my friends and family. It was the perfect little boost I needed.

I admit, it was difficult to watch restrictions in America and as close as England dial back to a point where performance was permitted. Up in Scotland, we weren't permitted to play background music in bars and restaurants as an attempt to reduce the need for people to shout and therefore spread Covid particles. I'm not sure what was worse – not having music when you're in a bar trying to get turnt or being able to hear yourself chew on a mozzarella stick in a silent restaurant. I'll let you be the judge of that one!

As far afield as Australia and New Zealand (who had managed to suppress the pandemic like no other country seemed to be able to do) they were able to perform *Chromatica* in clubs. I can't believe I let another drag artist perform 'Replay' before I got my hands on it. I'm fuming. Absolutely fuming.

Lockdown rules went back and forth a few times, but before long I was informed that we would be returning to the set very soon. My eyes were drawn back to the show immediately. I was focused, galvanized, and ready to return. Hot off two wins, I knew I had more to prove than ever. I wanted to come back from the pandemic with a vengeance.

The Second Lap

'Sorry I'm late, there was a leaf on the line!'

We were back. For a moment, it felt like we hadn't left. Walking in one by one, we took our places at the table and awaited our fate. Was everything going to be the same as last time? Covid had decimated the lives of so many people. Would we even know each other any more? It turns out that everyone had pulled through, relatively unchanged – except for a few millilitres of Botox. Wait a minute. I counted the heads. Seven? Where was Veronica?

RuPaul entered, after poaching one of Ginny's wigs before they left, and delivered the devastating news that Veronica had tested positive. Fear shot down my body. I hadn't known anyone personally that had contracted the virus – thankfully, my friends and family had dodged it over lockdown. Was she going to be OK? Not only that, but I simply cannot imagine something that is out of your control stripping away an opportunity like this. Hearing that she had an open invitation to return was reassuring, and I cannot wait to see her get the party started. Again!

Then the second lap began. The show must go on, as they say! RuPaul called in the Brit Crew, and in walked these big furry animals. They unmasked, and it was only Joe, Cherry and Asttina! Wait a second, we had to choose who was to come back? Fuck's sake . . .

I went with who I wanted to compete against the most. When I said earlier that Joe Black was a total legend in our community before the show, I meant it. She was so well established as a cabaret artist, known for delivering bone-chilling vocal performances and drop-dead looks. Literally. Drop dead. We became the two group leaders for . . . a pop-group challenge. 'RuRuVision'. I think the two of us were potentially the least qualified to lead girl groups. Picture this: Grans Aloud vs the SugaPensioners – 'Hobble This Way'. Not a good look.

It ended up going in a different direction, however. I tried to be smart with how I selected my teammates and selected who I could best envision in a pop group – Bimini, Tayce and A'Whora. I didn't know if any of them could sing, but I knew for a fact that we would look absolutely amazing. After a more than shaky (for me) recording session with MNEK, we took to the stage adorned in pink and orange. The United Kingdolls! I have to say, 'I like it rough but my lentils tender' has stayed with me since filming.

You'll never be lost at sea when you can climb aboard me! Inspiration can come from the strangest places. I was walking across the Clyde one day after I'd been confirmed for the show, and I saw a life ring and then I knew exactly what my 'Day at the Seaside' out-fit was gonna be. Orange and silver PVC, white fishnet (stoned of course!), embellished with arm-band sleeves. These were actually functional, by the way! All of this, topped off with a life-ring headpiece I had created myself. Disbelief struck again when it was announced we were the winners. A hat trick of wins! I don't think anyone expected big Lawza to come out of a girl-group challenge with a badge – I know I sure as hell didn't think I would. Dumbstruck, we took our places at the back of the stage. This episode was so memorable for so many reasons, but I think what takes the cake was Ellie Diamond trying to eat a shep-herd's pie through a seagull beak.

Can we skip on to episode seven? I don't think I'm quite ready to relive 'Snatch Game'. It's like this: Law-rence Chaney. The queen of a thousand faces. Known for performances as Maggie Thatcher, Melissa McCa-rthy, Davros, hell, even Mr Burns.

'Hello, Smithers. You're quite good at turning me on!'

Countless make-up re-creations from pop culture,

horror films, previous *Drag Race* alumni . . . in the bottom two. This was the episode I was most nervous for people back home to see, and watch. I had been told for years by friends that if I were ever on *Drag Race*, this would be the challenge I would take home for sure. I think I had let that build up into a huge fear of being a letdown, which ultimately ended up being my downfall.

After scratching off Maggie Thatcher from my list after Baga Chipz had done her the previous season, I went through my options. It wasn't easy – yes, I could do a lot of voices, but who could I do well enough to perform as them in a game show? Eventually I whittled it down to three characters. Susan Boyle, West Lothian's illustrious breakout singer superstar. Fanny Cradock, television chef of the last century who brought cost-effective gourmet food into the homes of thousands of Britons. Finally, Miriam Margolyes, thespian lesbian, actress extraordinaire, who had risen to recent internet popularity for her bold comedy when recalling stories from her life. Miriam, obviously, was who I went with.

I sat down on the panel, feeling flustered and stressed out. RuPaul introduced me and I started strong, but it was only downhill from there. I honestly knew it was coming when I landed in the bottom two with Tia. Watching the other girls killing it made it even harder to keep up. Despite wearing three badges on my chest, the insecurity was back with a bang. I'm very grateful for Tia, explaining that being strong doesn't mean not being human. This helped me dust myself off and get back on the horse.

Was the dream about to be over so soon? This was not what I had planned. I was in the bottom two and had everything to lose now. I quickly had to put the pity party to one side. The upset and fear turned into angst and determination. I quoted the famous Glasgow chant just beforehand, 'Here we, here we, here we fucking go!' and, bringing out my inner Braveheart, I fought for my position.

I won the lip-sync, even if it was at the expense of my kneecaps. Poor Tia was flapping around, dressed as a pterodactyl, and I was the meteor that took her out.

Reading sure is fundamental! The library opened, disposable reading glasses at the ready. I think my favourite read I gave was to Ellie.

'You are so stupid, you studied for your Covid test!'

Too soon? Convert trauma into comedy, that's what I say. I was so excited for the challenge, an unconventional material challenge! Raven also came round and gave us make-up advice, which I've taken humbly and still use to this day. While my initial plan of silver sportswear didn't quite work out, I knew better at this point than to get defeated. I quickly adapted and created a costume out of blue tarpaulin, orange strapping and some dusters. Lawrence of Chania was born!

The stand-up challenge was next, another challenge I was incredibly excited for. Ironically, I chose to talk about love and relationships, which, as you'll remember, I've had a bit of a rocky experience with. I had such a genuinely fun time with my routine and the best part – it was all bloody true! I beamed onto the runway in a *Doctor-Who*-villain-inspired pink crystal nightmare. This costume was so hard to get into – while it might have been a stretch fabric, it had so many stones and latex prosthetics that it wasn't movable at all. Lemme tell you, trying to get my lovely hourglass into that took up half of my prep time! I was gagged at the critiques. Comedy legends like Dawn French praising me on my comedic abilities. Like, *what?* The Vicar of Dibley thinks I am funny?!

I couldn't talk about this episode without addressing the elephant in the room. Ellie and I were very much at each other's throats. I should be crystal clear on this – basically, it's like I said on the show. Ellie and I were friends for a long time before *Drag Race* and had shared a lot of important moments together. Of course she was playing tactically! It's a competition and I totally understand that, but with my brain in panic mode and a fear of losing everything I had worked for, I spoke the first things that came to my mind. I'm not particularly proud of it. I was in a vulnerable place and put my guards back up.

Everyone gets emotional, it has to be said. There just aren't cameras to pick it up. While watching the show back, more times than I can count, I thought *Fuck, why did I say that?* We all make mistakes and I applaud anyone who can make peace with their fuck-ups and carry on. That's what life is all about – just be glad they aren't on iPlayer. 'Tenacity' and 'resilience' aren't just words that sound like team names on *The Apprentice*, they are key character traits that I needed to pull me through life.

Then it was the penultimate episode. This is when shit gets real – the top four become the top three. I struggle to even visualize getting so close to the end and missing out. First, we had the puppets mini challenge and a masterclass from the one and only Natalie Cassidy! We're just doing this now! Bubbly's in the fridge! My son is in the kitchen, eating a biscuit! For the challenge, I channelled my inner Melissa McCarthy in *The Boss*. I barged into the door with my turtleneck spirit-gummed to my chins as Phyllis Bitchell. I might have fumbled a couple of lines, but I managed to push through and unleash my inner East London bad bitch. 'Nothing gets past me, sweetheart!'

The message from my mum was the best boost I could have had to get my ass through to the end of the show. For the second-to-last time, I walked onto the runway in my best 'panto dame' look! Keeping the purple theme, I brought together mint and purple with pincushion sleeves. I crafted a replica sewing machine for my headpiece and completed the look with a measuring-tape belt. 'He's behind you!'

The *Drag Race* format works so well in the UK because we are completely comfortable with taking the piss out of ourselves. Drag is constantly ridiculous, and I was shocked that this season was so widely enjoyed because many of the challenges, guest judges and references were unique to UK culture.

I will be dozing off to sleep at night and suddenly Tayce's iconic 'YES, I AM!' line will be playing in my head.

This must be why this season was so successful: we really got into your heads, whether you wanted us there or not.

When I heard the first few beats of 'Last Thing on My Mind', I knew this lip-sync would be one to remember. Ellie and Tayce are two queens known around the UK for their high-energy dance performances. Ellie had never lip-synced until this point, but she was facing the lip-sync assassin who had managed to send three people home out of the original twelve. That's a quarter of the season! They turned out an amazing performance, and it felt right that they managed to score a double shantay.

The Finish Line Approaches

After we filmed the final episode, said our goodbyes to each other and went home, it was time for broadcast a few months later. Nationwide, we all sat down and pulled up the iPlayer at 7 p.m. sharp. Watching the show felt like being right back on set. I could remember exactly how I was feeling at each moment: my thoughts, damn, even the smells of the lunch awaiting me at break. Post Traumatic *Drag Race* Disorder, I call it. I'll speak more about my mental health later (that one's a doozy!), but every week I absolutely astral-projected right back to the studio. I don't know much about witchcraft, but if that's what astral projection feels like, then am no' interested.

Before long, it was time to go to the private finale screening. As Charity Shop Sue said in the crowning video (shout out, hen!), alternative endings had been filmed, so none of the finalists knew their placement – nobody did. For support, we could bring a plus-one to the private screening. While the others brought their mums, I was a little too worried about the pandemic to bring Big Phyllis, so I brought my flatmate instead. We took a particularly unpleasant Covid test – you'd think I would be excited to gag on something after so long – and I arrived on location with Kiko at my side, knowing that in just over a day it would all be over.

If I'm being totally transparent, part of me had given up hope. I'm a bit of a glass-half-empty kinda gal, so in this situation I was fairly certain that Bimini had taken the cake – and wouldn't have blamed them if they did. I sat back in my hotel room, taking in the high ceilings and mammoth sash windows. Mahogany panelling, plush carpets, sweeping twelve-foot-high curtains. It felt bittersweet.

A few hours after settling in, we were called for our

last supper. All of us sat around the table – Bimini, Tayce and Ellie with their mums, and me with Kiko. The passing of the peas seemed like the breaking of the bread. I looked around at everyone, predicting my loss (betrayal is a bit strong a word) and wondering if Kiko would thrice deny knowing me after going home empty-handed. I needed support, and once again it was Phyllis, my mum, that pulled through for me.

'You might be upset, and disappointed, but you aren't a sore loser. You all deserve it. You need to be a supporter.'

Dawn broke. All four of us had to put brush to palette and start getting ready – from morning till night we had press back-to-back. This was the day all fans of the show had been waiting for, the day we were waiting for. Usually, a full day in drag would exhaust me, but I was running on adrenaline (and cheese strings). Breakfast was brought to me, but it went cold on the table as we did interview after interview. The screen went dark on the final interview, and we had a couple of hours to ourselves before the big moment.

I sank into the armchair and looked across at Kiko. She smiled back but knew not to speak. Wait a minute, that sounds pure like I had scared her into silence! Jeezo, I don't mean that. I just mean that she knows me very well and knew that there wasn't anything that anyone could have said to calm my nerves at this point. I didn't know how to feel, how I was meant to feel. I couldn't decipher what was excitement and what was anxiety. Was it dread? When you're waiting to hear the all-important news that you've been waiting to hear for months, it's consuming. I'm sure you know the feeling. Gripping the end of the armchair, we sat in near silence for what seemed like an eternity. Then we got the tip to go downstairs.

This is the Beginning of the Rest of Your Life

We got into the lift and descended, not unlike my heart into the pit of my stomach. Putting one foot in front of the other was a struggle – and not just because walking in heels exacerbates my premature sciatica. Feather boa at the ready, I stepped into line with the other queens. Ellie, hair scraping the roof, in a baby-pink picnic-basket fantasy. Blonde mullet to the floor and arms encased in zebra-print gloves, Bimini, with her body wrapped in immaculate white. Tayce, with her signature black hair and an encrusted polka-dot coat that looked like it was twice her body weight. And then me, head to toe drenched in purple – hey, I started as I meant to finish!

Charity Shop Sue called our names, and we walked in and took our places. Glued to the seats, we waited for the screen to get rolled in and fix our eyes on the show. Behind the screen, in another room, sat Kiko and the mums. That sounds a bit like a band. Maybe they could be the next United Kingdolls, with their white wine in one hand and their other hand fixing that one bit of your hair that won't stay in place. Once again, 7 o'clock came, and the show began. The screen flashed with a montage of our highlights throughout the season, with our confessionals overlaid. Every single one of us deserved it, but only one of us would make it.

Seeing myself sat on that sofa, once again trying to write lyrics, and, apparently, choreographing sealed it for me. I . . . am not a recording artist. Cut to the Tic Tac lunch and listening to my story of where my drag came from and growing up in Scotland admittedly touched me. Everything I said to Ru and Michelle was true – I love London, I love travelling, but Glasgow is where my heart is. I promise I didn't mean to say no quite as quickly as I did when Michelle asked if I was going to move!

I damn near covered my eyes when it came to watching the choreography practice back. As I said in the episode, the last time I saw Jay Revell I started crying and couldn't dance for shit, and this time I was in fight or flight mode. Turns out that works, because this time around it wasn't as much of a struggle to get through to the end of the damn routine! When it came to the performance, however, I took it all in.

'Turn your frown upside down, and that's how you'll snatch the crown!'

Seeing the other contestants walk onto the stage at the

end of the song was also a very heart-warming moment. All of us on stage together performing (mainly) in sync was breathtaking, and the sisterhood felt very real. We are the cast of *RuPaul's Drag Race UK* Season 2!

As I watched myself walk down the runway for the final time, I thought about the preparation process, and all the people who came together to make this happen. It takes a village. This was actually going to be my promo look. However, we made the executive decision to swap the two looks last minute. It felt right to end the show in this gown. (It's another reason I don't regret branding myself with purple, because if I didn't, this wouldn't have been possible!) This look is a homage to RuPaul's iconic racer look from the 'Cover Girl' music video and the *Drag Race* promo. I wanted to put my spin on it and merge the worlds of new drag and old. A biker-style jacket with leather panelling and mesh juxtaposed with a floor-length fishtail and encrusted checkerboard felt like the perfect way to make that happen.

Hearing the dreaded poignant music and the picture of bowl-cut wee Lawza almost broke the dam protecting my make-up from absolute ruin. There's something deeply emotional about reflecting on your younger self and speaking as if it was to them. You're always told to look on, look ahead, focus on what's next, but looking back can make you realize how much you've been through to get to where you are in that moment. Always take a moment and consider all the difficulties in your life and how you've got past them and pat yourself on the back – it's a vital step on the journey to self-love. I'm annoyed because I forgot to tell my younger self one thing. McDonald's now deliver!

On saying that, though, I really do need to take my own advice to relax a bit more, because at this point in the night it felt like my veins had jammed themselves closed. I was beginning to get lightheaded, my heart was pounding, my corset felt like it had my lungs in a vice grip and wouldn't let go. In less than twenty minutes, we would cross the finish line. Elton John started playing, and we all watched, unable to look away at our last chance to prove that one of us was the UK's Next *Drag Race* Superstar.

The song ended, the music grew quiet, and Ru spoke the crucial words.

'I've consulted with the judges, but the final decision is mine to make. The time has come to crown our queen. The UK's Next *Drag Race* Superstar is . . .'

Everything went blank. Her lips moved, but I didn't hear what came out of them. My brain somehow didn't connect what my eyes saw and what my ears heard. My name? No, she didn't say my name. I was just about ready to stand and applaud the winner when the confetti cannons went off behind me and everybody began screaming in my direction. My ears were ringing. Everyone was looking at me. It hit me, harder than any bully could, harder than anything ever had before. Ru had said 'Lawrence Chaney'. Was that my name? That . . . was my name!

Crowned Queen

Can someone go through the five stages of grief in half a second? Let me tell you, hen, the answer is yes. Except this feeling wasn't sadness, it wasn't anger, it was happiness. Pure, unexpected, untainted happiness, mixed with a lethal dose of surprise. I had talked myself out of being in with a chance so violently that I genuinely didn't think there was a universal timeline where I managed to achieve my goal and walk away as the crowned queen – but I had. I had done it. The weird kid who loved food that little bit more than they loved jogging had triumphed, finally.

The dam holding back my tears had well and truly broken. My vision blurred as I cried like never before. This was a kind of crying I hadn't experienced previously, though. The tears were truly happy tears. Ellie was crying as she applauded, Bimini threw her hands into the air and cheered, and Tayce was on her feet, jumping, with a 'Bam, bam, bam!' I couldn't see this, however. I only managed to surmise it from watching the video back.

It's almost a black-out moment. In the most positive way possible, you forget how to function entirely. I couldn't breathe, see, hear, speak. You thought Kim

Kardashian was an ugly crier? Kim, meet Lawza Chaney. Everyone was on their feet. The room was spinning, it was all a total blur.

After the moment had subsided, Bimini ran to get her phone and immediately took a selfie and had a moment with me. Ellie was still a blubbering mess and Tayce was just happy to be out the house. Kiko had run over and grabbed me tight, impaling me on her five-inch, steel-spiked choker.

'I'm so proud of you, we're all so proud of you. You've done it, you've actually gone and done it!'

We all reset and took our places, walking one by one back into the room with spark cannons alight, for the runners-up to receive their QBEs. There it was. Glittering in the fittingly lavender lights, the crown and sceptre.

I picked up the sceptre, turned to the camera, and thrust it into the air.

'For all the Scots out there . . . FOR FREEDOM!'

Could You Be Next to Enter the Race?

If you are looking to follow my hoof-prints on your own path to stardom, one of the best ways is finding that uniqueness, nerve and talent and trying out for the show yourself. It's not the only path to success, and not everyone is destined to walk that path, but if you don't try then you'll never know!

There's no secret formula on how to get cast. No cheat codes, no shortcuts, no hints, or tips – other than this. Be yourself. A massive element of *Drag Race* is exploring your drag character, your past and your future. Authenticity is the key, always. Don't under-estimate the challenges that you may face, because it's definitely not a walk in the park either. Often, in the face of adversity, any façade will fade away and you'll be left with your tail between your legs. Don't get caught out! Be true to you.

As you know, one of the biggest reasons I wanted to win the show was to show young queer kids that their hometown didn't need to be a hindrance to their aspirations. I feel like I've done just that. Don't let anybody ever tell you different. Never become disheartened by obstacles or rejections either. It's a gigantic cliché, but everything happens for a reason. As we say in Scotland, wit's for ye won't go by ye!

Assuming that you shoot, and you score, I would like to suggest some potential porky-pies for your sudden departure. These are best used on your family and your boss – only people that absolutely insist on a reason for your absence. Honestly, if you're going to use one of these absolute bangers, do it over the phone unless you've mastered the art of the poker face. Depending on how gullible your target audience is, you can afford to have a lot of fun here!

Excuses to Use If You Need to Make a Surprise Disappearance – Dos and Don'ts

DO say:

- ✓ 'I'm away to *Coach Trip*, Brendan's oan the phone.'
  Nobody remembers Coach Trip *any more, so they'll just smile and nod when you tell them.*
- ✓ 'Babes, I'm just fucking off for a bit.'
  This one is good because it's vague and a very reasonable thing to do.
- ✓ 'I've got a residency at Butlin's.'
  This is not a gig to be sneered at. I know performers who would pay good money to see their name in the dim lights of a caravan park.
- ✓ 'I've been cast as Fat Bastard in the *Austin Powers* reboot.'
  This will only work if you are fat and Scottish, sorry.
- ✓ 'I'm rehearsing for *Shrek The Musical*.'
  This may also only work if you are fat and Scottish, sorry.
- ✓ 'I'm Elaine C. Smith's body double in SuBo's new biopic.'
  *This will only work if you are fa— *ahem*.*
- ✓ 'I'm going Down Under.'
  British people always fuck off to Australia when they've not got anything else going on, so this is one of the strongest and most believable excuses.

✓ 'Lorraine Kelly has asked me to be her make-up artist.'
This is a gig nobody in their right mind would turn down.

✓ 'I've had enough of drag, I'm going to do a degree in hotel management.'
Management degrees are where hopeless academics go to die, so this explains the disappearance perfectly.

✓ 'I'm going on the Romanian version of *Big Brother*.'
Big Brother *doesn't air in the UK any more, so you should get creative with it. Provided you don't know anyone from south-eastern Europe, this should work fine.*

✓ 'I'm going to see a man about a dog, and a woman about a bussy.'
The first part of this phrase is generally used to excuse an imminent departure — adding the second part personalizes it to yourself and adds to the credibility.

✓ 'I'm taking a drag sabbatical. Honestly, I'm shattered, Sandra.'
Every now and then, an overworked and exhausted Brit will piss off for a year and travel the world (or at the very least, the Outer Hebrides) so you can count on this to excuse a long period of absence.

DON'T say:

✗ 'I'm going to be one of the people that are away to trial living on Mars for a bit.'

*Just saying you're off to Mars probably won't work —
everyone knows you can't afford that. This excuse
would work if you said that you're Elon Musk's
personal competition winner and maybe then you could
be on your way to the big red planet.*

✘ 'I've won the lottery – I don't need to do drag
any more.'
*The logistics of this are a bit slippery. You might have
drag weans popping up left, right and centre, claiming
you're their mother, wanting their rightful inheritance.
This excuse may also make local tax men begin to
salivate, so unless you want the wolves at the door, you
might want to avoid this one.*

✘ 'Haw, mind your business, hen. I don't ask
what you're up to when you're on a two-week
bender.'
*This just sounds like you're shagging a straight guy
who is having a fortnight of curiosity.*

✘ 'I'm making like my dad and fucking off.'
*Dad, if you're reading this, this one is for other people
to use. I know you didn't fuck off, Nick. Big respect
to you. Don't use this one if, like me, you actually
have a very supportive father.*

✘ 'Remember that fine I got for indecent
exposure in public? Well, I never paid it, so
now I'm doing six months in the jail.'
*This one will only work if you're known for
the odd nipslip or twelve – hopefully you're not, so
I've put this in the don't section. Are you known for*

indecent exposure? Are you reading this from Barlinnie?!

✗ 'I'm on a social-media detox.'
This is probably not a great excuse — queens only do that for twenty-four hours, then the FOMO takes over.

✗ 'I'm getting my third nipple removed. It's huge, the surgery is going to take months.'
I'm sure a third-nipple-ectomy is a huge and trying surgical procedure. However, I'm not quite sure if it actually exists.

8
That's Pure Mental (Health)

If you can't swim and end up drowning in the sea, you need a lifeguard, don't you? Mental health is like that to me. Most people have ups and downs when it comes to mental health. A great amount of hindsight and reflection on past events in my life has highlighted many times when my grip has slipped. These days, I use that reflection to keep a close eye on how I'm doing. Overcoming embarrassment and shame to allow yourself to lean on close friends and other external assistance is so important.

Being more open about when you're not in the best place means that you can get the help you need to get you back on the straight and narrow. The world would be a better place if we were more transparent on how we're feeling – it's better oot than in! The journey to becoming the best version of yourself is less like a race with a start and finish, and more like an everlasting cycle. Feeling down or depleted is OK – your feelings are perfectly valid – and learning to recognize those feelings has helped me immensely. Get the Kleenex out, this chapter might be a tearjerker.

Young, Dumb and Full of Crippling Mental Trauma

I don't regret the negative or traumatic experiences I've been through. In my opinion, they've helped me to grow and evolve into a more resilient person with a thicker skin. You've heard me talk about my school experience already, and the notorious bullies.

Even though contemplating my time in both primary and high school has led me to be thankful for those encounters, I do wish that I'd been able to help myself better at the time. The naivety of childhood can explain a lot, and if I hadn't closed up so quickly then perhaps I would have been able to cope better.

Despite being a queer person blessed with a stable home life when I was younger, I still didn't think I had an outlet. This was nobody's fault but my own. Confiding in my parents didn't feel like an option for me – it felt like an admission of weakness. For some reason, at a young age, I tried to deal with things myself. Learning how to be independent like this can be a gift in adulthood, but it was far too early for a child to try and cope alone. Babes, if you cannae tie your shoelaces and still need to wear Velcro shoes on the school trip to Rothesay, then you're probably not ready to take on the ramifications of isolation and harassment by yerself.

Like I said earlier, at school, I had it all. Shouted at by passers-by, tripped over in corridors, tied to trees during lunch breaks (that actually happened, by the way), and called a fat ginger cunt. I have previously derailed that accusation, but once again for clarity – I am not ginger, and never have been. Where the hell did they pull that from? Is it only in Scotland that your natural hair colour is an actual reason to bully someone? Naturally, that treatment left me with a bit of a complex, and although there were some people that helped me make it to the other side, when moving on to further education I had still failed to deal with what was going on in my head.

The Chaise-longue

With my guard firmly up, I started studying at the City of Glasgow College in 2014. I wasn't willing to let anyone in and very much kept myself to myself – every day, I told myself that nobody liked me. My mind was pretty much made up about that before I'd even met anyone, to be honest. Please don't misunderstand, I wasn't purposefully putting these thoughts into my own head, it felt involuntary. The adversity in school had trained my brain into simply expecting negativity from every situation. You'd think studying acting would teach me to at least put a brave face on and get on with it, but perhaps not. And no, celebrity impersonation wasn't a module in the course – sorry, Miriam Margolyes.

I eventually worked up the courage to divulge my issues to my mum. While I had struggled to do this throughout childhood, college initially felt similar to my school experience, even though there was none of the active harassment and victimization. Hell slap it into me, I had to do something. She suggested that I try out Cognitive Behavioural Therapy (CBT). I'm really thankful to have the parents I have, because they have no stigma against mental-health problems. My mum always encouraged me to speak my mind and open up, and once I managed to push myself to do so, relief washed over me. It was a massive weight off my mind to have someone listen to me, understand and offer up a potential solution.

Up until then, I hadn't considered counselling as something that I might benefit from. There were, and still are, a lot of stigmas around it. Tropes surrounding mental illness in the media suggest that your entire world has to be crumbling to end up sat in front of a therapist. There is so much fear surrounding the process, and because people are ashamed to admit they need a bit of help, they end up suffering in silence. Many of us don't feel comfortable with the idea of sharing our deepest and darkest secrets with a total stranger, which is understandable. Talking about the media stereotypes involving mental health . . . why is it always a damn chaise-longue? Do you know how hard that word is to say for someone Scottish?!

Reconnecting the Dots

Sometimes, when you try to join the dots in a picture, you get it wrong. CBT trains you to connect them in a better way by helping you recognize patterns of unhelpful behaviour and better coping mechanisms, as well as pointing out faulty thought processes. A lot of the time, it's about trying to focus less on what gave you the lasting problems, and more on the present and what's in front of you at that moment. This kind of therapy is sometimes the best way to start when looking for techniques to help you get through traumatic experiences. It's like a good colonic – it clears you right out.

I ended up sitting in front of a fantastic counsellor – not on a chaise-longue, may I add – and the work began. We spoke about my fears and insecurities, and some methods I could use to face situations that I would usually run away from. We discussed how I could keep calm in a variety of situations and think them through rationally. She also worked to help me better understand the motivations of others.

One specific scenario comes to mind. My peers had

found out that I could make costumes and do make-up, and soon enough they were asking me to help out with the wardrobe for college productions. I was really wary of taking them up on their offers. When I spoke to my therapist, I explained how I thought they were taking the piss out of me. I was really confused as to why they wanted my help. If they didn't like me, why would they want me to do that for them? My counsellor simply said, 'Well, do you like making costumes? Do you think you're good at making costumes? Aren't they simply seeing your talent for this, and asking you because of that?'

I realized then that they had been complimenting me all along and I allowed it to build my confidence. After a while, I accepted that they were actually reaching out and extending the invite to be my friends. My past experiences had led me to become a bit cynical, to the point that I couldn't take genuine acts of kindness at face value. I was reading into situations far deeper than necessary, ending up in a totally negative state of mind.

When my therapist laid it all out to me and presented the information in a different way, that's when I began to become aware that I was shutting myself off, rather than others shutting the door in my face. Laying everything out plain and simple, as well as the counsellor helping to lead my thought process in another direction, helped clear the fog that was clouding my vision. It's almost like you're in a mental maze and keep taking the wrong path. CBT helped me to choose the right way forward. It was a total lightbulb moment.

'Hawd on a minute, these people are my pals, they aren't going to kick my head in!'

After my block of sessions was over, I felt like I could finally start living my life as an adult. I was studying in a new city, away from all of those people who had made my life hell, and I wasn't going to let them take away another second of my time.

It's important to mention that I was incredibly lucky to have been able to access therapy through college. It's hugely inaccessible to so many people – the NHS waiting lists can be long, and private sessions can cost you an arm and a leg. Now, more than ever, we need access to mental health care that is safe, reliable and high quality for each and every person who needs it.

I no longer feel like I need to prove myself or put on a persona to protect myself. While you see a character when I'm in drag, it isn't fake, or a barrier like before. It's all me, to varying degrees.

Drag is the Best Medication

My mental-health struggles have a lot to do with why I took to performing in drag so quickly. I think some people's next question when they hear this is, 'Aren't you putting on a mask and hiding away?'

Far from it, in my opinion. Calling it a mask feels like the wrong metaphor – I see it more as a superhero costume. If you choose to, you can still be yourself, except a supercharged version. Not many superhero costumes involve a bright orange feather duster, but you work with what you have.

Previously, I spoke about how my weight had fluctuated over the years, and the impact of the comments people would make about it – how I was better looking when I was thinner, or even just comments on weight gain in general. Weight-related self-esteem problems are a very heavy topic (pun intended), and they do take time to decode and figure out. Drag has played a massive part in moving me to the point where I am proudly plus-size. Yes, I wear floor-sweeping gowns, corsets and padding, but I'm no stranger to a pair of pasties and a dream. The risks that drag encourages you to take help you face the body-dysmorphia thought process and grow to love the skin you're in.

The media rarely show role models that don't fit society's beauty standards. However, in the world of drag and cabaret, there are countless entertainers to choose from that are proud of their plus-size bodies – and too right, missus! Humans come in a variety of shapes and sizes, and finding role models in the world of the performing arts helped me and so many others to fight back the thoughts that we were 'made wrong' and don't deserve to feel beautiful. If you told me a couple of years ago that I would be wearing curve-hugging jumpsuits and transparent latex dresses, I would have told you to go away and bile yer heid!

Another great method I like to utilize (and have tried to throughout this book) is converting trauma into comedy. It's a very cathartic process for me! While some things might be inappropriate to make light of, I am comfortable enough to take the absolute piss out of my own experiences.

It's like this: I've written these anecdotes about the adversities I have faced because the vast majority of them had a negative effect on me in some way. Some-where down the line, these events were huge, and I was very fearful of them. Converting those happenings into something to laugh at plays a huge part in minimizing and compartmentalizing them, therefore making them easier to cope with. Plus, it gives me a filing cabinet's worth of content for my next stand-up routine! It's a win—win!

Social Media: the Arena of the Twenty-first Century

Ahh, the fickle mistress that is social media. Isn't it concerning how something made to connect the people of the world together could drive them apart so much? Social media is the source of many modern-day mental-health issues, for children right up to adults – and I'm no different. The internet is the twenty-first century's answer to gladiator arenas. Twitter, Instagram, Facebook, YouTube ... All these platforms have played host to some of the fiercest feuds I've ever experienced.

Take Twitter, for example. While you might watch two middle-aged Karens fight over their begonias in the Facebook comments, or come across Richard's YouTube channel where he tries to tell you that the gender wage gap doesn't exist, Twitter is where it goes down. Trying to have a nuanced discussion when you have to condense an argument into 240 characters isn't particularly effective and will often end in raised tensions. That might actually be the understatement of the year.

Needless to say, when the promotional campaign for *Drag Race UK* Season 2 came out, I struggled. Landing my dream gig aged only twenty-three was one of the best moments of my life, but also unfathomably terrifying. I was used to the regular audience I had in Scotland. I knew the crowds, the performers and the venues like the back of my hand. Being thrust onto a global platform overnight is an experience like no other. All around the world, I was being surveyed, critiqued and judged online, before even opening my mouth.

It was a challenge to take it all in. Gaga once said, 'There can be 100 people in the room, and 99 don't believe in you, but one does.'

Well, this felt like there was 100,000 people in the

room, and 99,999 didn't believe in me. Obviously this was not the case whatsoever, but the self-doubt from my college days was back in force. It's difficult to receive hate based on your appearance alone, and I hadn't learned the unspoken rule of not reading the comments quite yet. Some comments in particular somehow managed to hit on every potential insecurity I could have possibly had. My dress was too basic, my hair was out of proportion, the construction of the belt didn't make sense . . . I wasn't exactly expecting to be liked by absolutely everybody, but seeing every last element being put under a microscope was a total shock to my system.

A few weeks later, my less-than-pleasant encounter with Ellie aired. I was watching with my flatmate at the time, and I had to leave the room. She gave me the update afterwards, but nevertheless, later in the week, I watched it for myself. It was uncomfortable, to say the least, and Twitter was alight within minutes. My phone would crash from notifications, which I eventually had to turn off so that I could unlock the damn thing. Seeing other people give their opinions on what was such a vulnerable moment for me took me past my limit, and I had to get out. I deactivated my Twitter account and deleted the app from my phone. Sometimes the best thing to do when there isn't a solution to a problem is take some time away and regroup.

It goes without saying that Ellie and I are back to normal now. We've spent plenty of time touring together after the show – one that stands out in particular is 'Ooch Aye . . . the Tour' from back in June 2021, in which we travelled around Scotland in what felt like a victory lap around our nation. We had local performers in every city, and for many of them this was their first gig back after things began to open up again in the summer. Having matching wigs and costumes and performing an opening duet with the Scottish sister that experienced the rollercoaster of *RuPaul's Drag Race* with me felt correct.

During the whole experience, I leaned on my friends that had helped me prepare. They reassured me constantly, and I'm immensely grateful for their time and efforts putting me back together. To everybody who has shown me love right from that fateful day, I thank you, and I apologize for allowing the insecurities to creep back in.

After some of the fear and doubt subsided, I was able to feel excitement for the fast-approaching finale date. It was either excitement or apprehension. Or just really bad acid reflux. (Rennie, if you've got a PR list, now is the time to reach out.)

Pressure Cooker

Reality TV can be really intense. It's a bit like a poppers hit, but it lasts for a few weeks. Your head's pounding, you don't know where you are or what's going on, and you're surrounded by homosexuals, but . . . you adjust.

Believe it or not, I honestly didn't think I cried that much until I watched myself back on the show. Intense situations can make mental-health problems that you've previously overcome rear their ugly heads again. If this ever happens to you, please don't lose heart and think you've undone all your hard work. Working on your mental state is an everlasting cycle, and at *Drag Race* my eye was on so many things at once that I forgot to keep it in my headspace.

Coming out after half a year's isolation and going back to the show, for some reason my feelings of loneliness had continued. Others in the competition had begun to feel there was favouritism afoot. I can only assume they had arrived at this conclusion based on my challenge wins and the way RuPaul said my name. No matter what I managed to pull off, I still told myself that the others felt I was winning because they thought I was Ru's favourite, not because I deserved the achievements. I started to second-guess every positive comment made by the judging panel and fixate on any critique. Highly strung doesn't quite cut it . . .

Despite the headspace I ended up in, I would be lying if I said there weren't plenty of moments when the other queens gave me support throughout filming. In those lucid moments, I was able to remind myself of where we were and the extreme amounts of stress everybody was under. As time passed, I was able to bring back more and more of my positive coping mechanisms and get my feelings under control. Being able to finish a challenge, then sit back and say, 'Well, fuck, babes, it's oot my hands now!' was truly liberating.

The other queens got me out of my own head and I was able to look at myself from outside and see what was happening. I cannot thank my Season 2 sisters enough. That was ours to experience together, and it'll for ever be a shared memory.

Hindsight is Humbling

A big part of looking after your mental health is practising gratitude. I've been blessed with so many incredible opportunities, and my determination and resilience has allowed me to make the most of them. There are hundreds – no, thousands – of incredibly talented performers who just haven't yet had the opportunity to showcase their star power to the world and I am so grateful that I was one of the lucky ones. After spending so long dwelling on the fact that maybe I wouldn't be able to do drag in the same way for a long time, I have so much gratitude for those that have got me to this point. It was a team effort, and a bloody fantastic one at that. This huge feeling of thankfulness is humbling and has played a big part in getting me through the pandemic and continuing in my career. Drag and performance is returning all over the country and maybe that means my quarter-life crisis can be put on pause for the time being.

Mental health is something that, while intangible, is very much present in every waking moment of your life. Everyone experiences moments of extreme happiness and euphoria, moments of emptiness and hollowness. That's pure mental. Taking care and watching over your psychological and emotional wellbeing is one of the most important things you can ever do – it's equally as important as your physical wellbeing. If I don't look after the old noggin, then I can't fulfil my duty on the planet. I have a responsibility to show young queer kids what they can achieve if they set their mind to it, no matter where they're from. I need to be a role model for those embarrassed about being plus-size and show them that we have nothing to hide. All in all, looking after yourself should always be a top priority.

Mental-health Dos and Don'ts

✓ **DO** keep watch over your wellbeing. Mental-health issues can strike anyone at any time. Previously dealt-with problems might return. If you go through a rough patch, never feel ashamed of it, and always seek the help that you need, whether that be from family, friends or a professional.

✔ **DO** take a step back every now and then. Throw yourself into everything head first and, at some point or another, you're going to give yourself a concussion. Pausing, regrouping and taking stock can help you to stay on top of things, and potentially save you from burning the candle at both ends.

✔ **DO** laugh at life. You know how the saying goes: laughter is the best medicine. Going through a low point? Laugh. Missing your friends? Laugh. Burst haemorrhoids? Laug— wait, actually, that'll probably make it worse. Maybe get that one checked out.

✘ **DON'T** spend your life poring over social media. There are some right grumpy bastards on there! Social media is better used casually, if at all. Connect with your friends more personally, through a text or a phone call.

✘ **DON'T** be afraid to cry. Something I learned, after crying for nine out of ten episodes of *Drag Race*: if you're going to cry, you're going to cry. There is absolutely no benefit to holding it in, because it will, I repeat, IT WILL find a way out. Usually through your tear ducts.

9
Sisterhood of the Travelling Pads

The other drag artists in your life can make you or break you. You'll come to realize some gals are your friends and some you're just never going to see eye to eye with. Thankfully, I've always had those sisters who have made me whole again when I thought I was breaking apart.

That sentiment is why it's so important to acknowledge that one of the most fundamental elements of drag is sisterhood. Forging, maintaining and sometimes losing relationships with your drag sisters can be some of the most memorable experiences of your existence, and your career!

From the dawn of gay time, we've relied on our community to get us over the tough hurdles that life throws at us. I am no different. *Drag Race* has changed the landscape for a lot of my relationships and myself in general. The transition from local queen to RuGirl can be rocky, and relationships can evolve and sometimes end. It's natural for things to change with time, especially when you've gone through such a big change yourself.

Season 2 Sisterhood

When you're all stuck in the same room, going through the experience of *RuPaul's Drag Race*, it tends to bring everybody closer together. After filming, and even more after broadcast, however, everybody becomes very busy and more distant from each other. Trying to maintain your social life when you haven't stopped for months on end can be impossible.

One thing that works to remedy this is touring. While we may have had a slow start due to Covid, when we managed to reconnect together at events across the country, dwindling fires of friendship could be amped up again. Ellie and I toured Scotland; Asttina, Cherry and I toured England; and I've done a few shows with Tayce and Ginny. Not to mention the United King-dolls! I've been able to reunite with almost everybody from Season 2 through shows and performances.

I'm really glad that the friendship between Ellie and me didn't change after the show. Our disagreement on the show drove us apart a little, and again when it was broadcast, but our ties of friendship run deeper than this. We're both Scottish — we get each other and understand how our scene works. We have so many shared experiences that it would be a shame to leave it behind. Not only are we from the same country, but we were both the first two from Scotland to walk onto *Drag Race UK*, ever. That'll never change.

I've forged a close connection with Tia Kofi since *Drag Race*. We did butt heads on the show, and ironically our friendship pretty much started from her elimination onwards. I think an intense head-to-head situation like that either drives you apart or makes you closer. I know where I stand with Tia – she's a very straightforward, honest and open person, and I really respect and vibe with that. The music she's released since the show is insane. We also share a government name, of course, which led to a bit of confusion during our lip-sync. Someone from the back shouted, 'Yes, Lawrence!' and I think both of us must've assumed it was for us.

When you think about it for a second, though, it does seem rather unlikely that someone would've shouted someone's legal name at them while cheering them on. Cue 'Mad World', with the black-and-white slo-mo. Sorry, Tia.

I would say Joe Black is my other closest friend from the show. We knew each other briefly beforehand and were rather excited to see each other. I have to say again, I was absolutely devastated when she was eliminated not once, but twice! Even Joe's witchcraft couldn't break the curse of coming back and then immediately going home again. We speak regularly, and despite my royal dislike for gin, I bought some of her limited gins when they were released. That's what true friendship looks like. Slap your name on a bottle of gin and your pal buys it. Friends for ever.

I guess what I'm trying to say is that even though there are arguments and catfights on the show, that's totally normal. It's a crazy place to be in, and emotions run high when exhaustion and pressure set in. Even though we're not all in constant contact with each other, we're all still sisters for ever.

Get Out of the Shade

Life after the show, with the local scene, is very polarizing. A lot of people have opinions about you that they may not have had before, now that they've seen you on national television. I think that having both Ellie and me on the show at the same time, and for both of us to make it so far, made a lot of people feel the need to pick a side. Not only that, but past friendships I once had have now faded. Before, everything was community-based and you could be acquaintances with 700 people all at once, whereas now I feel spread thin and have closed ranks a little. It can be lonely, but the maintenance of multiple friendships and a high-pressure career feels unfeasible together.

I had a run-in with a local queen I met recently. From the outside looking in, it might look like after coming off the show you are untouchable. I can absolutely assure you, this is far from the case.

'Oh, your make-up looks nice. Thanks for trying today! Did you try because I was coming?'

'You need more energy. You need to pick it up – unless you were faking it on TV!'

This was an awful lot of shade for someone I'd never met before. Normally, there's a bit of a shady back and forth, but this was someone I'd never spoken to, on- or offline. It's almost as if, these days, people are more inclined to make a nasty comment to greet someone (which is generally a missed stab in the dark at insult humour) than a pleasant greeting or compliment. If you want to make fun of me and have a bit of shady banter with me, that's fine. However, this didn't feel like that whatsoever. The comments were generic, and there was no actual introduction. The thing is, shade isn't for everyone. Not everyone is built to handle that, nor does everyone have the quick wit and humour to avoid coming off as insulting. You have got to be able to take it back, especially when making a dig at me. She messaged me afterwards with a 'Nice to see you!'

I thought, *Was it? You didn't act like it.*

I'm not asking you to blow compliments up my arse, but you don't need to degrade my confidence in a failed pursuit of comedy; the crippling anxiety is still alive and well without your help!

I've also noticed in the past few years there is a

specific 'compliment' going round: 'You look good . . . today.'

What is this?! Is it meant to be shady? Is it genuinely just a compliment, and I'm misreading the slight pause? Why are we so desperate to get these little digs in? When you actually get to know someone, you can read them for filth, but I can't see the point in slagging queens you don't know. There is no point going to a gig and going home feeling worse than you did when you were hate-crimed outside.

The Intent Behind Words

I did experience some tension from people who I once called sisters after going on the show. When you start to gain notoriety in the local scene, and even more after being on a platform such as *Drag Race*, your voice and opinions have a lot more weight. Things you say have more influence and people are more inclined to choose to agree or disagree rather than choose to ignore. When you mention them, it matters more, following them means more, promoting them means more. This can end up in some situations being misread, and a multitude of misunderstandings.

I was interviewed by a Canadian queen, Wilma Fingerdoo, on Instagram Live. We were discussing pay for drag artists, and she was telling me that she can draw a lot of parallels from her own scene to the

Scottish scene and our predicament. One pro that Canada does have over the UK, however, is one-dollar notes. While their performers can get tipped more often as it's in smaller amounts, largely audience members in the UK do not tip this way as our notes don't have as small a denomination. We cannae just ask people to lob pound coins at us unless we want to end up in Accident and Emergency with a burst lip and a nosebleed.

Wilma asked why I thought pay was quite as bad in Scotland, and what could be done to improve it. I tried to be measured and honest with my response. There are so many people nowadays that want to do drag with the advent of *RuPaul's Drag Race*, and this is amazing! I love how people are finding solace in performance and becoming more comfortable with themselves through drag. However, I think it would be rather difficult to make immediate and significant change to pay because of the sheer quantity of drag artists nowadays. The problem is there are 200, if not more, drag artists in Glasgow, and very few queer clubs across Scotland, and not all of them actively book local drag shows, so the scene is diluted.

It means that asking for a pay rise may become difficult because somebody newer may do the gig for a fraction of the price in the name of getting experience – which is perfectly understandable! However, for truly significant change to be made, clubs either need to alter their practices organically because they care, or a fully unified front of drag artists must essentially put their wigs down and strike. Am no' talking about lobbying outside these clubs – I mean unanimously agree not to accept fees under a certain level. There are people who do drag solely for fun, and people who want to make it into a full-time career.

The other factor that comes into play is experience. Some drag artists will be naturally more expensive than others and may end up losing out on work if they alter the fees that they usually work for. At what point are they meant to increase their fee? What is the standard for that fee? Not only that, but sometimes an entertainer will improve faster than others, so years of experience might not have as big an effect as one might think.

This caused a stir amongst some newer artists in Scotland, as they misread my answer as a complaint about the uptake of drag these days. I believe the issue was with my use of the word 'diluted', and I totally understand why that might have a negative connotation. I wasn't implying that there was a reduction of quality, more that the sheer quantity makes things significantly trickier. There are literally not enough clubs or gigs to go round just now – the numbers just don't add up.

This situation ended up bringing larger issues to the forefront within some friendship groups that I had. We became divided, and it was sad to see friendships of over five years come to an end. This might not apply to this specific situation, but a lot of the time a hive mentality can be very real. Either that, or people can be heavily swayed to believe a different point of view before actually asking about the true intentions behind what you might have said. It's incredibly upsetting how fickle some relationships can feel – we as a community face so much adversity in this world, yet somehow sticking together is really hard.

A New Kind of Exhaustion

It's generally uncommon for a local artist to be working more than four nights a week – even then, those that landed that many regular gigs in Scotland (pre-Covid) were doing pretty well for themselves. This contrasts to a schedule like mine, where in a span of four weeks I may have five or six days off. Even on those days off, I have meetings, merchandise to organize and costumes to design and order. The schedule is brutal sometimes.

Due to this, a lot of the time I need to really conserve my energy to avoid total exhaustion and becoming unwell. Returning to local shows with this new technique was jarring initially, because I was always known for being up for a good laugh and joke backstage at every show. I wasn't afraid of necking a couple of shots and dancing the night away either, but unfortunately that just isn't realistic any more, and I think this has put a lot of people in an awkward position.

I was chilling backstage at a show where Alice Rabbit and I were reunited. I think she misread my chill as a low mood, when in reality I was mentally preparing myself to get on stage, grab that mic and perform my heart out. She kept trying to pick me up (not physically, don't worry), dancing around the room and cracking jokes at me. Alice seemed disheartened when my reactions were a bit more lacklustre than usual. She asked if I needed a Red Bull. God, if I had taken a Red Bull, that would have fucked up my precious four hours of sleep that I ended up getting that night. It was like she thought it was her responsibility to ensure I was at 100 per cent energy, 100 per cent of the time. While I understand she was looking out for me because she is a good friend, wanting to make sure I didn't feel like shit, any sort of attempts were futile.

I was exhausted from travelling, not necessarily from a low mood. If I'm a huge ball of energy backstage, it ends up impeding my ability to be a huge ball of energy onstage. It's a shame, because this really has made working with my friends different. While things might have been a bit more relaxed and fun before, I can't help but come off rather serious and quiet backstage nowadays. To any of my friends who may be reading this, it's not you, hen! I'm just tired, please don't worry! Please, please don't give me Red Bull because it won't wake me up, it'll just make my heart race at an uncomfortable speed!

The Luxuries of Living

After being on the biggest stage for drag in the world, returning to a small two-bedroom flat in Glasgow was . . . strange. You'd think as the winner I would be immediately living it up in some sort of townhouse in the city centre, but, honestly, I'm rather conservative with money and quite careful where I spend it. We outgrew that flat very quickly – it was already barely large enough for two drag queens, and it's definitely not big enough for a drag queen and a *Drag Race* queen.

During the show prep, our living room was constantly overrun by our other friends sewing or embellishing. There were fabric and scraps everywhere, sequins ingrained into the carpet and pins everywhere. Our wig wall got larger and larger, before it was essentially a wig corner. It made for quite a high-stress living environment, because there really was no escape from anything as both of our bedrooms became filled to the brim with clothes and belongings we had cleared from the living room. There was no longer a communal space that wasn't being used for storage of some kind.

That essentially continued after the show. Wardrobes

got fuller and fuller, cupboards were filled with suitcases bursting at the seams, and every surface had some precarious stack of something on it. Trying to keep on top of housework was impossible and led to raised tensions. The concept that your living environment has such a strong effect on your mood is very, very real.

While Kiko has offered me invaluable support over the span of the last couple of years, I do struggle to navigate some aspects of our relationship now. We applied for Season 2 at the same time, and I remember thinking about how I would feel if she was cast and I was not, and what that could do to our friendship. Scratch that, what if we were both cast? We would be pulling in favours from the same circle of people. It was a huge fear of mine, but obviously the opposite happened. I have to say, she took it really well, and my casting over hers didn't seem to affect us whatsoever.

Being someone who speaks so publicly about how anything is possible and chasing your dreams to the ends of the earth has presented a new problem, however. While I have become a RuGirl, she is still a local drag artist with hopes of being cast on the show one day. She has a residency with Trigger, as I once did, and yet now our day-to-day lives have become so different. I can't fill her head with delusions and hope, I have to be realistic and honest. The duality of that is totally fucked, because what I say publicly is truly how I feel, but it would kill me to build her hopes up only for them to be dashed if she doesn't achieve them immediately.

I am lucky that Kiko, like myself, would rather hear the honest truth than a sugar-coated lie. I can give straightforward, raw critiques, and she does not take it to heart. She's very self-aware and understands why my choice of wording may be different for her than for the general populace. Our sincerity and integrity with each other lead me to believe that our friendship will stand the test of time, even after we inevitably go our separate ways and move out. She's a good cunt.

Truth and Transparency

I've said many times that I value straightforward truth in my friends. It sometimes may not seem like that, as my self-consciousness can present as defensiveness at first. However, in the long run the people I need around me are those that are going to tell it like it is.

I find that people who are rather far along in the journey of self-discovery are often the best for this. They know who they are, and what's what. Anyway, what's the point in filling my head with delusion and lies if they're just not true? Friends like that always have good intentions but run the risk of inflating someone's ego to blimp-like proportions. And listen, hen, when you're already dangerously close to those proportions in the body, having them happen to your head as well is nae fun!

Openness and transparency are other qualities I value greatly. Someone that can talk candidly about their experiences often helps me to feel more secure and trusting when it comes to talking about my own.

Alice Rabbit once said to me, back when I had braces, 'Your lip-syncing is really off. Has anyone ever told you that?'

My braces were causing my lips to hook on to them and I wasn't able to enunciate and lip-sync correctly. She would give you feedback raw, even when you didn't ask for it. If you asked her, 'Was my performance shit?' she would say, 'Aye it was.' (If it was, obviously!) Alice wouldn't leave it at that, though. She would impart advice on how to improve. It was constructive.

Alice taught me many things. She showed me that with performance mixes, it's all about building. You wouldn't start with a rave song and then finish with a ballad. She is also plus-sized but holds her own when it comes to dancing and high-energy numbers. You would hear about Alice before you met Alice. People definitely felt threatened by her success, and she became quite a polarizing figure – unapologetically so. She knows exactly who she is and tells it how it is.

Kiko is another person whose self-discovery has

allowed her to give a very honest and measured point of view on many issues. After being shot down previously when I was trying to explore and discover my gender identity, Kiko's experience with her own gender helped to bring that conversation out of the box I had put it in, at the back of my mind. Seeing her be transparent on so many occasions when she came out about being a transgender woman, and bluntly truthful about the realities of that, helped to open my eyes to many of the societal struggles and pressures when you don't identify with the gender you were assigned at birth.

Having more of these difficult conversations with your friends, whether they be about honest truths or deep secrets, ultimately works to strengthen the friendship. Please don't misunderstand. I don't mean just turn round to your pals and start reading them to filth! What I'm getting at is that when your friends create an environment and bond where you can be honest and open with each other without fear of serious repercussions, the relationship strengthens immensely and you're both totally better off for it.

Ultimately, drama and shade aside, it's most important to me that we have each other's backs. We all have an unspoken respect for one another, but maybe it should be more of a spoken respect. I'd like to encourage everyone to set that change in motion. I want to uplift and empower my sisters and any new performers that arrive on the scene. Life is too short to hold grudges in our community. We have enough people who want to see us fail without having to add to that ourselves. C'mon, let's lift each other up.

10

Next Stop, Hollywood!

Heavy is the head that wears the crown. When I imagined my wildest dreams coming true, I didn't consider the pressure that comes along with it. That crown is heavy and if you're not careful it can really fuck up your spine, so I'm trying to look after my posture. I am lucky to be surrounded by people who uplift and support me. My family, friends and fellow queens offered me an unimaginable amount of praise and guidance after the show ended. However, when you win a show like *Drag Race* you are thrust into a world of stardom and excitement that you don't quite have enough time to adjust to. Suddenly, Cara Delevingne is in your DMs!

I still live in the same flat I've lived in since 2017 – the blue tick doesn't change that. It's got a leaky kitchen tap and a bathroom ceiling that is one push away from falling in. I am very glad to be busy at a time when many people have struggled to maintain job security and I don't take a moment of this for granted. I just need a little more time to get used to it.

I have been working non-stop since the finale of the show aired. I'm a total perfectionist, so I struggle when I don't have complete control and autonomy over every job I do. This industry isn't made for control freaks like me. I need to be comfortable with turning up without a clue what's going on and giving it my best. I've struggled to decipher which opportunities are best for me, especially when I am wary of people's intentions and cautious of my drag career's lifespan. There's no *How to Be a Successful Drag Queen for Dummies* book. Well. Not until now!

Looking to the Future

Very soon, I will no longer be the reigning queen of *RuPaul's Drag Race UK*. This has created a ticking time-bomb feeling. In this fickle showbiz world, fame is fleeting, so I'm petrified that I might not have the same opportunities in a year's time. I'm trying my best to cram it all in. I'm up to my eyes at the moment but still I don't want to say no to anything in case I miss out on something. I've got major FOMO and this whole experience has only heightened it.

One thing I'm glad about, though: I don't have to chase venues for a pay cheque myself any more, which is a massive fucking relief. Sometimes I've caught myself thinking, *Was working in retail really that bad? I mean, sure, it was dreadful at times, but at least I didn't have a sixth toe developing out of the side of my calloused left foot.* Of course, I'm talking absolute shit. Retail jobs are torturous and designed to break sixteen-year-olds' spirits as they join the world of work. If I ever need to sell another zip to a sixty-year-old that comes in looking for satin lining to re-upholster her son's beanbag . . .

Fame vs Anonymity

The safety blanket of anonymity no longer exists for me. The feeling of notoriety or fame is as overwhelming as it is thrilling.

When the show was airing, my flatmate and I jumped to my local Tesco. I had my hood up and a mask on, feeling like I was in incognito mode. Everything seemed to be going well initially . . . I got through the dairy section (putting half of it in my trolley), got a wee meal deal or ten . . . Clumsily enough, I walked into a sign. What?! Winning *Drag Race* really fucks up your depth perception. Anyway, the sign fell to the ground, and someone rushed over to help me pick up the display.

I looked up and said, 'Aw, thanks very much, hen.'

Her eyes lit up. I thought she thought I had robbed her or something, but lo and behold – 'Oh my God, is that LAWHRENCE CHANEEH?!'

I still got clocked by a fan of the show. This was the first time I'd experienced being 'spotted'. It's a crazy experience when you are peacefully browsing the Lidl bakery and faintly in the distance you just hear 'LAAAAAAAWHRENCE CHAAAANEEEH!'

I'm getting used to this part now and I really enjoy connecting with fans of the show. So far they have all been really kind and supportive, nobody has chucked a bottle of piss at my head (yet). It's strange to be asked for selfies in the street when you are at my level of 'fame', so I can't imagine what it would be like for the bigger stars who have been dealing with this for years. I'm no' Justin Bieber, but the day I set foot in a Glasgow queer bar for the first time will be a sight to see.

I love talking to people that recognize me in public, but something I haven't really gotten my head around is those that want a picture with me OUT of drag. Rather than having a conversation with me, the first priority is getting a selfie with me, even though I'm wearing carbonara-stained joggies and have no eyebrows within three miles. But as I write this, I realize that they don't just want a picture with you because you're that drag queen off the telly.

Because of *Drag Race,* people have been able to see more of me as a person, so I see that there's no pressure to constantly be in drag 24/7. I don't feel like I'm letting people down any more by not donning the sequins twenty-four hours a day.

Maybe this is just part and parcel of my desired career path. I don't want to sound like one of those celebrities that are like 'Poor me, I have all this pressure and also a fuckload of cash in the bank, life is so hard.' I'm at the very beginning of my career, so I can't even say I'm loaded or that I face the same amount of pressure as some A-listers. Ask me again in a few years. I might make it to the C-list by then.

Social-media Wars: the Trolls Strike Back

When I won the show, I made sure to stay away from social media for a bit. I didn't want a stranger's negativity or opinion to ruin the moment I'd waited my whole life for. Audiences have their favourite queens and queens have their die-hard fans. There were a lot of comments online telling me that I didn't deserve to win or that I'd taken the crown from a more talented queen. It took me a minute to get my head around it all.

So, I won this show, chosen by the judges, but I'm the one getting flak for it?

I can easily slip into the self-doubt mindset, but this time I wasn't going to let it happen. I nipped it in the bud by focusing on the opportunities I had lined up for the next few months. Sometimes you have to just get that tunnel vision on and block out the haters. Social media has allowed people to hide behind a faceless profile and hurl abuse at strangers online with no consequences.

During the broadcast of *Drag Race*, I admit I had let it take a toll on me. I was a people-pleaser and wanted to be universally liked. I think that can be quite a common trait amongst entertainers. After deleting my Twitter, the time away from my phone helped me realize I don't have to rely on the opinions of others to get by. This is how I see it now. It's a two-way street. If I'm allowed to celebrate my win, others are certainly allowed to be upset that their favourite didn't win. I cannot police their emotions, but subsequently they cannot – and will not – police my happiness.

I don't take these things personally any more. When people told me that I didn't deserve to win the show, it was like that saying: water off a duck's back. I know I deserved to win that show because every finalist standing on that stage deserved to win it. Besides, runners-up on reality television competitions often surpass the fame and kudos of the winners. I am the self-proclaimed Susan Boyle of *Drag Race* and remember SuBo didn't even win *Britain's Got Talent*! I guess that makes me more of a Michelle McManus after winning *Pop Idol*, than a SuBo . . .

Life after the Race

It has been a whirlwind journey since January 2021, when we exploded onto the nation's screen on *RPDRUK* Season 2. Still in the throws off the coronavirus pandemic, it was nice to offer a bit of fun and laughter to all the fans out there. Many people watched the show for the first time ever on our season and we've now got an even bigger family than before.

It was odd to be introduced to the world overnight whilst sat at home. With restrictions still in their highest tier, there were no live shows, photoshoots or press conferences. Fans of the show have said that our season helped them get through the pandemic, giving them something to look forward to every week. What they don't realize is, it's what got me through it too. The distraction of the filming process followed by the thrill of seeing the public react so positively gave me the boost I needed to get through one of the most trying periods of my lifetime.

It was so fun to see people engage with the show and see everything we had been keeping secret for so long. I didn't expect to be received so well. Normally, a plus-size queen is put into a certain box, and the general fanbase seems to overlook them – or, for want of a better term, sleeps on them. Gaining some celebrity fans along the way was another plus. I had well wishes sent to me from my nation's patron saints, Michelle McManus and Lorraine Kelly, amongst many more.

Everything happened at once and I didn't really have time to soak it up. As life has only got busier, I still don't think I have. I've had a few different television gigs recently in which I've met a whole load of notable UK stars. I'm often asked if I get starstruck and the answer is: not really, babes. I would treat you the same if you were Kim Woodburn or Kim Kardashian.

From a young age, I attended conventions and events which often had appearances from some of my favourite television and film stars, and back then I would freeze up and just smile and wave. I met actors from things like *Doctor Who*, *The Avengers* and *Star Wars*. Hindsight on this has shown me that I was probably losing out on what could have been some very valuable and memorable conversations. Take Katy Manning, for example, one of the OG *Doctor Who* companions – she played Jo Grant. She was so lovely, but I was just a speechless bag of nerves. I could have been asking her how to make it in the biz! I've always thought I'd make a great Doctor . . .

I've been lucky to have really great experiences with everyone I've met since the show. Overwhelming support and congratulations have been coming my way and I'm incredibly grateful and appreciative. My schedule is hectic, though, and sometimes there is little room for a personal life on this schedule. Often, one-off shows or trips can turn into a three-week stint away from home, so I've found myself up at the crack of dawn to get some new underwear from Primark without getting papped.

The pressure of maintaining your career post-*Drag Race* is very intense. You initially compare yourself to the other girls. I have found myself watching what other queens have been doing after the show and holding it up against my own schedule. You see the tweets: 'I'm on set today.' Aye, I'm on set as well – sadly it's onset diabetes but surely that still counts for something.

Seriously, though, how do you not compare yourself to these other talented drag artists? Audiences are constantly comparing you, so it's natural that you end up doing the same sometimes. It can seem like you're wearing George at ASDA and they're wearing Jean Paul Gaultier. The comparisons can make you feel like you must want everything and be visible everywhere. How many ads can you have? How many TV appearances? If you let it, it's stops being about the quality of the work and starts being a numbers game.

Being in the spotlight can mean that invasive thoughts have a way of snaking in if you're caught off guard. *Am I getting as many gigs as a winner should?* You've just got to bat them away and keep doing what you're doing. I want to tour for the rest of my life, even though it's knackering. It's what I'm good at. I have a lot of things planned in the next few years and I can't wait for you all to see them.

When I tour, I never want it to seem like it's a final hurrah. I've got plenty up my sleeve, and any other orifice you can think of. In fact, I would quite like to alter a popular joke: the only thing that'll be left after the end of the world is Cher, cockroaches and the

Chaney! You won't be getting any farewell tours from me any time soon!

Touring can feel quite gruelling but it's all about building up stamina and learning how to do make-up, sew new outfits, write new routines, learn new songs and mixes – all in a tour-bus toilet. On most occasions, you need to travel on the same day as the performance. If you had any plans in between shows, you'd better cancel because you've got to shower, shit and shave before getting ready for the show.

There was an unfortunate incident where I forgot to pack underwear for a tour. For three weeks I washed my boxer briefs in a sink with warm water and soap. I don't want to give away too many industry secrets, but they stank of barbecue beef Hula Hoops. Enjoy your lunch.

I want to highlight the contradiction with what people imagine when you say 'I'm off on tour!' They think it's luxurious, imagining five-star hotels and an entourage carrying a little dog behind me. In reality, you're living out of a suitcase in an EasyJet cargo hold. You're wearing the same outfit over and over again. Your wigs are crispier than your teenage cumrag and you are so hungover you don't know if you'll be able to hold your breakfast down, let alone a mic.

Whenever I am in a new city and place, I want to make the most of it, I want to go and see shows and see the local performers. I want to see Veronica Green singing 'Get The Party Started' and feel it echoing inside my arsehole. I really make the effort to get out there.

If you just wake up, work, then go straight back to sleep when you're travelling to so many different, wonderful places, life feels so boring and beige. You'd be missing out! Drag lives should be anything but beige. We are every colour of the rainbow and I want to keep that alive, no matter how much I want to crawl back to my Jurys Inn after a gig.

Touring can be a very isolating experience. You're constantly surrounded by people, but it still gets lonely. It's an odd thing. As a comedian, I find myself in a room (half) full of people who are laughing at my jokes . . . but I still end up feeling weirdly solitary. When you're known for telling jokes, it sometimes feels like the weight of the social baton is heavier. My mind is going at 700 miles per hour, trying to make everyone else feel comfortable in the moment, sometimes forgoing my own personal comfort.

Even when I'm not performing, I spend my full day being talked at by people at meetings, shoots and events. Chats can feel one-sided, and more statement-based, and if nobody stops and checks in with you, you end up spending your whole day talking with a million people but having a conversation with no one. It's important to remember, though, that this is all absolutely just internal pressure that I'm putting there myself. Nobody is purposefully trying to outcast me or not ask me how I am. It's a mindset I'm working to change constantly.

Scottish Stardom

I end up missing Glasgow deeply when I'm in London. London has essentially become my home away from home – it's where I've probably spent the most time since winning, after Glasgow, of course. I love being there because of the proximity to my drag sisters, and because it feels like a whole country in one place. That has a huge downside, though . . . Everything is too spread out! You can't walk from A to B without it feeling like running a double marathon. For context, A is my hotel and B is the local McDonald's. Jokes aside, in Glasgow I can get anywhere in twenty minutes or less. In London, a two-mile journey translates to a three-hour Uber journey. I hate it!

As you'll well know by now, I am proud to be born and raised in Scotland. Can you imagine? Someone came down from Scotland and smashed it! And not *just* Scotland. Helensburgh, a wee seaside town with no points of interest. When I told my school I wanted to be famous, they gave me work experience in a kitchen. God forbid they let me anywhere near a theatre. Scotland is a very patriotic nation and I am not shy about that. I am proud to be someone who proved we can make it anywhere, even with the thickest accent.

I spoke about it earlier, but most people who make it move away. I'm adamant that success doesn't only mean living in London. I might have a lot of work down there but I'm just as keen to create opportunities and enrich the industry right where I am. It is funnelled into us from a young age that Scottish people don't make it to Hollywood, and if they do, they have exceptional circumstances. It's a one in a million chance. There is a lot of pressure from the industry to move to London. I think the problem is that some people forget there is a world outside of the capital. All over this country there are amazing, talented people who are being overlooked and miss out on the opportunity to thrive. Give us a chance and we'll show you what we are made of.

Holyrood to Hollywood

So what's next for Lawrence Chaney, I hear you ask? The sky is the limit, babes. Will I be the next Angelina Jolie? Probably not. I am still a work in progress at twenty-four (years old, not twenty-four stone), but I'm so excited to travel the world and entertain people. My own mother is going to have to start booking in a slot for a cuppa with me at this rate. I don't have plans to slow down any time soon.

I will be filming my own television series in Hollywood right after writing this. That's right, I didn't just get three badges and a crown . . . I got three badges, a crown and a Hollywood TV series, thank you very much, World of Wonder! I've always fancied my name in lights, so this next venture seems very fitting to my fantasy.

Opportunities will come and go, and who knows how long they will last, so I'm grabbing them by the baws. If this is my fifteen minutes, I'm going to milk it for all it's worth. Above all, I want to continue making people laugh, whether that's on my stand-up comedy tour or on the telly.

The ultimate dream would be my very own talk show. I can just picture it now: *Awrite, Hen, with Lawrence Chaney*, on every morning after *Lorraine*. I can even see Lorraine having me on as a guest presenter, no bother.

Mind how I was talking about drag maws? Well, Lorraine feels like my showbiz maw now. She gives me advice on everything and is always only a text away. Hell, it was because of her that I got verified on Twitter – half a year after I won! I come to her for all the advice I need.

My ideal talk show goes like this . . . I'd have Gemma Collins doing the weather, Nigella showing us how to whip up a meal in the *microwavé*, and Natalie Cassidy doing the showbiz updates – the possibilities are endless. I'd invite on a variety of high-profile guests and ask them the all-important questions, such as 'Is my dress blue and black, or white and gold?'

I've been obsessed with daytime television since I was a wean. Most teenagers would be bunking off school to play computer games and get stoned, whereas I was skiving so I could watch Alison Hammond, Janet Street-Porter and Trisha Goddard. In hindsight, that sounds like a trio I'd like to share a joint with.

I got the chance to work with Netflix earlier this year with fellow *RPDRUK* winner The Vivienne, which involved watching TV and talking shite. This was the absolute dream. Imagine doing that for a living? I do it for free every day (but don't tell them that). I fancy my chances on *Bake Off* as well. I'd like to see me having a right good go on an empire biscuit. I'm only going on if Mary Berry makes a return, though. I want her to inspect my soggy bottom. Can we bring *Coach Trip* back? What is Brendan doing these days anyway? I feel like it's almost an obligation for me to go on, after using it as my 'going-away' excuse. Anything that revolves around me doing a lot of talking. I have been blessed with the gift of the gab.

One of my biggest aims in my career is to create change in the fashion industry. The fashion industry and fat people have never been a good match historically. People seem to think fat people can't wear fashion . . . I'm sorry? Lawrence Chaney was on the

BAFTA Red Carpet Best-dressed List, and she's not done yet.

I'm tired of seeing so much effort and creativity being put into fashion for smaller sizes only. Every single one of us, from XS to XXXL, deserves the opportunity to wear couture and express their personality through their clothing. Have you ever tried to express yourself with clothes from a shop called Big and Tall? No wonder I make my own!

Some people argue that my looks all have the same silhouette. Spell 'silhouette' before you criticize my silhouette. I call it branding. I hate when people base your value solely on visuals. I am not a worthless human being because you don't like what I'm wearing! I want people to realize there is money and beauty in dressing plus-size people. It's worth the effort to expand your mannequins and pattern blocks in your fashion label. Fashion is a universal language, and we all deserve to speak it.

More than anything, I want to continue to inspire small-town kids to glue on their nails and reach for the sky. I hope I have proven by my *Drag Race* journey that you are allowed to aspire bigger than your hometown and the mentalities of those around you. You are allowed to think *Maybe I can be the next Joan Rivers*.

You know I love to crack out a cliché, but it's true when they say it's all about what you've got on the inside. Where you're from has nothing to do with it and I'll never stop continuing to prove that. I'm nowhere near finished with my journey from Holyrood to Hollywood, and I can't wait to paint the rest of the world PURPLE!

Acknowledgements

Behind every good queen is an army of gays and gals and a solid support network. I wouldn't have made this book or had this career without these people, so thank you all.

To my mum Phyllis, dad Nick, sister Tamsin — I wouldn't be where I am without you.

RuPaul — you made it all happen and I am for ever grateful. To Thairin, Sally, Matt, Bruce and everyone at World of Wonder — you're all legends!

Paul Black, thank you for being a professional clown and confidant.

Conor MacDonald, Kim Khaos, Paris Ettamol, Kiko, Axel Aurora, Kelsay Higton, Joana Silvestre, CJ Banks, Niall Nicholson, Perry Cyazine — you all helped me prepare for *Drag Race* and I couldn't have done it without you.

I feel so lucky to have been supported through this process by the brilliant Transworld team, in particular Helena Gonda, Sharika Teelwah, Becky Short, Ella Horne, Sophie Bruce and Beci Kelly.

Finally, I'd like to thank all of my Season 2 sisters – and an even bigger shout out to my Season 1 *Drag Race UK* sisters, cuz we're all stealing your gigs!

Picture Section Acknowledgements

All photos are courtesy of the author except for:

Page 5, top: Lawrence at the launch of BBC Scotland (BBC Scotland/Alan Peebles)

Page 7, top: Lawrence and Lorraine Kelly at Student Pride (Aaron Hargreaves)

Page 7, bottom-left: Lawrence at the BAFTAS (Tim P. Whitby/Getty Images)

Page 8, top and bottom: The finals of *Drag Race UK* (World of Wonder/Guy Levy/BBC)

Glossary

Throughout this book I have been my real, authentic Scottish self, so in order to make sure you know what I'm talking about (and, as I said, to keep the suits at Penguin happy), I've created a glossary for all you lovely readers. This should help you get to know me a wee bit better. There are also some classic drag terms that some readers may not be familiar with. I want you all to read this book in all of its glory, and yes, that even means you heterosexuals. I also hope that you learn some new phrases and implement them into every waking minute of your life and, in turn, help Scotland and, more importantly, me take over the world. Enjoy, babes!

A:

Aboot: about
Aff: off
Am: I'm
An': and
Arse: buttocks

Aw: all

Aye: yes

B:

Barlinnie: HMP Barlinnie, the largest prison in Scotland

Bawbag: a scrotum. Generally used to describe somebody ignorant or obnoxious

Beat (your face): to blend make-up

Bile yer heid: boil your head, Scots way to tell someone to piss off

Bump: to steal

Bussy: a man's anus

C:

Cannae: cannot

D:

Dingied: ignored brutally

Doon: down

Douche: the sacred art of cleaning one's anus before anal penetration. Or you would call someone this when they are being a bit of a cunt

Drawers: traditionally understood to be a method of storage, but in Scotland, your knickers

E:

Editorial: as in: very high-end look, like a fashion magazine

F:

Fae: Scots colloquialism of the word 'from'

Feart: afraid

G:

Gagged: to be so surprised that you can't speak, as if you were gagged

Glesga: Glasgow

Grindr: an app for gay men to forge real, genuine romantic connections (shag)

H:

Haw: see: hawl

Hawd: to hold something

Hawl: an exclamation, equivalent to 'Hey!', or 'Oi!'

Heifer: what would be regarded as a heavier, bigger individual

Hell slap it into me: Scots way to say hell mend you, it's your own fault and you need to deal with the consequences

Hen: term of endearment, usually for a woman or girl, but can be applied to any gender

Hetty: abbreviation of 'heterosexual'

Hinging: the morning after the sesh where you feel like you've been hung out with the rest of the washing, limp and lifeless

Hunners: hundreds

Hunty: a combination of 'honey' and 'cunt'

I:

Isnae: is not

K:

Kabussy: see: bussy, except exciting
Karen: a term to describe someone acting entitled, usually asking for the manager at any establishment
Ken: to know, or have knowledge about
Kiki: a social gathering

L:

Lace front: a specific variety of wig that is tied with transparent lace to the scalp

M:

Masc: abbreviation of 'masculine', i.e. the oppposite of myself
Maw: mother
Megabus: a UK transportation service, believed to have once been used by Amanda Lepore
Mug: face

N:

Nae: no, none
Naw: no
Ned: a Scottish term for 'chav'. An acronym for Non-Educated Delinquent
No': not

Noggin: head, or brain
Noo: now

O:
Oan: on
Och: a Scottish interjection of regret or surprise
OG: someone who is exceptional, authentic, iconic, original
Oot: out

P:
Padding: material added to hips/bum to create a more feminine shape
Pals: friends
Papped: paparazzi'd, unconsensual photo-taking, when one is photographed doing everything from picking your nose to going to the supermarket, from slaying the red carpet to taking a shite
Patched: an alternative way of saying 'dingied'
Patter: style/content of speech
Pied: to be given the proverbial 'pie' – being ignored in an abrupt manner
Pish: urine/rubbish/nonsense
Pished: to be particularly inebriated with alcohol
Poof: derogatory slur for gay men
Pube: a pubic hair

Q:
Queerdo: like weirdo, except queer

R:

Raging: absolutely furious

Reading: the art of insults, originating in ballroom culture

Riddy: an embarrassment

S:

Sesh: a night out/a party

Shagpipes: bagpipes, except sexy

Shanner: something that is 'shan', meaning an embarrassment, a shame, or something that is dilapidated physically and/or unfit for purpose

Shite: faeces/particularly bad

Shiv: a homemade knife or razor

Shoap: shop

Skint: to be rather short on finances

Slagged: to be made a fool out of and mocked

Sleep: to 'sleep' on something is to overlook or ignore it; think: Lady Gaga, 'Artpop'

Snatched: when one's wig flies off of one's head

Sound: someone who is kind/good to be around

Stoning: to painstakingly, one by one, place rhinestones onto something, generally a garment/ costume

Stoating: walking ungraciously

T:

Toerag: a worthless individual

Turnt: getting turnt is to go out on the aforementioned sesh

Twinks: thin, young, gay men

W:
Wae: with
Wanky: pretentious
Wasnae: wasn't
Weans: children
Wee: small/a little
Wit: what
Wummin: woman/women

Y:
Yass: a term of enthusiastic approval
Ye: you
Yerself: yourself

About the Author

Lawrence Chaney isn't just the people's princess, they are the reigning Queen . . . of *Drag Race UK*.

Lawrence hails from Glasgow, Scotland but has exploded globally after winning *Drag Race*. This is their first book.